THE
POTTING SHED PAPERS

THE

POTTING SHED PAPERS

Charles Elliott

FRANCES LINCOLN

For Carol again

Frances Lincoln Limited
4 Torriano Mews
Torriano Avenue
London NW5 2RZ
www.franceslincoln.com

The Potting Shed Papers
Copyright © Frances Lincoln Ltd 2002
Text copyright © Charles Elliott 2002

British Library Cataloguing-in-Publication data
A catalogue reference for this book is available from the British Library

First Frances Lincoln edition: 2002

ISBN 0 7112 2009 3

Printed and bound in Great Britain by
Butler & Tanner Ltd, Frome and London

2 4 6 8 9 7 5 3 1

CONTENTS

INTRODUCTION

ONE OF THE MOST SATISFYING things I've learned in the seven or eight years I've been writing about gardening is that you don't have to be much of a gardener to do it. Of course, if you aspire to be a real guru, like Christopher Lloyd or Penelope Hobhouse or Anna Pavord or any number of seriously skilled horticultural authors, you do need more than a passing interest in the technology, if I can put it that way – you must know how to propagate plants and make them grow happily, how to design a garden, how to identify and be utterly familiar with a vast range of rooted organisms. Writers like these are in a position to instruct and inspire, working from within, as it were. Fortunately, however, there also seems to be a place for those of us content merely to potter around the subject, peering in from the outskirts, happy to explore its more curious, amusing and unexpected aspects. Because like any other human pursuit – and more than most, I've found – gardening is amazingly rich in history, anecdotes, strange byways and unusual characters. That, and not advice about pruning, is what you will find here.

Most of these pieces were written for the American magazine Horticulture, with no higher intention than to amuse myself and the odd weary gardener taking a break from spreading compost and killing tomato hornworms. Their miscellaneous nature is no accident. Though from time to time I've toyed with the idea of writing a proper joined-up work of garden history, a good story or a colourful personality will always distract me. This may, I know, lead to general incoherence, but incoherence is the nature of the world, and most of us have learned to live with it. Please try.

As will soon be apparent, I am an American. But I live in London and garden on the edge of Wales. This arrangement is peculiarly pleasant, not least because it gives me an opportunity to make use of some of the world's nicest libraries, especially the London Library and the Royal Horticultural Society's Lindley Library. Their wondrous resources are all the more attractive for being open to browsing, and I am deeply grateful for access to them.

One of my favorite titles has always been *The Diversions of Purley* by the eighteenth-century radical politician and amateur philologist John Horne Tooke. Tooke's work, a study of the origins of language, was highly popular but incompetent; according to some authorities, it actually delayed the introduction of scientific philology into Britain by decades. But to me the title has a charm that makes up for the book's shortcomings. The word 'diversions' suggests exactly the right mix of amusement, obsession, and evasion of daily responsibility. So if you want to call these essays 'diversions', I'd be delighted. Like gardening itself, they shouldn't be taken too seriously.

PLANTS IN PARTICULAR

The Lost Orchid

IN A COUPLE OF WEEKS OUR ORCHIDS will be peeping up out of the grass in a corner of the orchard. Every year there are a few more, purple spikes four or five inches high that you must hunt for. They are early-purple orchids, what Shakespeare referred to as 'long purples' in Ophelia's bouquet, and are relatively common. 'Relatively', of course, is the operative word here, because no orchid growing in the wild is really common, in England or anywhere else. When we consider the more glamorous tropical orchids, moreover, true rarity is the word.

As far as I know, no British orchid has ever been found, named and described, and then lost again, vanishing into a limbo of speculation and legend from which it may or may not ever emerge. Among tropical orchids, however, this has happened more than once. For nearly fifty years, for example, a *Paphiopedilium* called *P. fairieanum* was lost. It had first turned up in a London sale room in 1855 and was exhibited and admired at a Royal Horticultural Society show. But it could not be propagated and, in spite of a £1,000 reward, could not be located in the wild again. A band of surveyors eventually came across it once more in Bhutan – in 1904.

The best case of a lost orchid, the really classic case that brackets the whole era of 'orchidomania', is that of the spectacularly beautiful *Cattleya* known as *C. labiata vera* – the last word (meaning 'true') tacked on by frustrated botanists to distinguish it from the many near relatives found while it remained lost.

The famous 'tulipomania' that swept Holland in the seventeenth century saw collectors bid up the price of rare bulbs to bankrupting levels. While it never reached quite that degree of hysteria, a similar craze agitated horticultural circles in nineteenth-century England. This time it involved orchids, and was stimulated in the first place by the accidental import, to a gardener living near London, of some pieces of root and stem that struck him as interesting.

In 1818, William Cattley, like most people at the time, apparently knew little about tropical orchids, although examples had been trickling into the country at an increasing rate for nearly a century, brought by explorers like Sir Joseph Banks. How to grow them was a mystery. With no knowledge of their original habitat, nurserymen tended to plunge them into tanbark for the sake of warmth, and keep them as damp and airless as possible. Yet being epiphytes, which live a semi-parasitical life far from the ground on the trunks or branches of trees, most of them predictably faltered and died under such treatment. Mortality proved to be so great, in fact, that a few years later Sir Joseph Hooker ruefully called England 'the grave of tropical orchids'.

Cattley, however, had better luck with his specimen (which, as was much later learned, is one of the easier orchids to cultivate). It had turned up as packing material in a box of lichens sent to him from Rio by a naturalist named Swainson. In the autumn of 1818, Cattley managed to bring it into flower. It was, he exclaimed, 'The most splendid, perhaps, of all Orchidaceous plants.' The botanist John Lindley, agreeing, published a description and named it in Cattley's honour: *Cattleya labiata* (due to its pronounced lip).

As collectors in the field got busy searching for more *C. labiata*, its reputation spread. The few available divisions from Cattley's original plant gradually died off until there were none left. Rare examples mysteriously turned up from time to time at auction, bringing higher and higher prices – in 1870 £31 (the equivalent of £1,300 today), in 1880 39 guineas (£1,800). Meanwhile, other kinds of tropical orchids arrived – from South America, Southeast Asia and India, Africa, Australia – many of them exquisite. Rich connoisseurs eagerly followed the example of the Duke of Devonshire and his unparalleled collection at Chatsworth, vying with each other for the finest and most unusual plants. Dealers hastened to supply them. Propagation being difficult if not impossible, this meant sending orchid hunters out to likely locations and taking plants from the wild.

It is difficult to imagine the scale on which this was done. Vast areas were denuded, not only of orchids but of the trees that bore them, chopped down so that collectors could reach the plants. A single expedition to Colombia in search of *Odontoglossum crispum* felled 4,000 trees to collect 10,000 orchids. In 1878 one London dealer announced the arrival of two consignments containing a total of two million plants. Entire orchid-rich areas of Central and South America have been without orchids since. There were a few voices of protest: 'This is no longer collecting,' said the director of the Botanical Garden of Zurich, 'it is wanton robbery.'

Amid the destruction botanists did at least learn more about the orchid family. Where in 1823 only 134 species were known, in the year 1837 alone 300 new species were introduced. (In 1852 Lindley would estimate the total in existence to be about 6,000 – and this was an underestimate.) But of the precious *C. labiata*, nothing. Swainson had not been specific about the place he found Cattley's plant, though it was assumed to have been somewhere near Rio. In 1836 a naturalist named George Gardner, working in the Organ Mountains 15 miles inland from Rio, found what he thought was the right *Cattleya*, and collected it 'with much difficulty and no little danger' from the edge of a precipice. Unfortunately, Gardner brought back only a few living plants (which were probably the wrong ones anyway), and by the time professional collectors got there the site had been stripped for charcoal-burning and coffee plantations.

Orchid hunters found other *Cattleya* – *C. mossiae*, *C. mendelii*, *C. trianaei*, *C. dowiana* and others. Against the usual odds of tropical fevers, bandits, unfriendly locals and lack of transport, they collected the plants and shipped them off to London and Paris, where the few that survived went to auction. But no *vera*. From time to time one would come to light in the glasshouses of rich men like Lord Douglas-Home and Lord FitzWilliam; two appeared in the London Zoological

Gardens in Regent's Park (the theory was that they had something to do with a shipment of South American monkeys); the Imperial Gardens in St Petersburg flowered a few, but the director didn't know or wouldn't say where they had come from. All this time, as auction prices for rare orchids soared, dealers kept urging their agents to locate the precious *Cattleya*. Competition between orchid hunters was intense, sometimes brutal, frequently involving spies and sabotage. (A favourite trick: pay a dock worker to urinate on a shipment of packed plants, causing them to bolt en route and be worthless on arrival.) By the 1860s, thanks to Lindley's research on habitats and the horticultural skills of the Duke of Devonshire's great gardener Joseph Paxton, growers learned ways of cultivating higher altitude cool weather species, and a flood of Andean varieties entered the picture. But that *Cattleya* still beckoned. Frederick Sander, the principal orchid dealer, with huge storehouses in England and Belgium, had his men scour the Rio area, follow Gardner's and Swainson's tracks, and hunt through every plausible part of Colombia and Venezuela. One man spent five years tracing the coastline of Brazil, without luck.

The sort of excitement involved in the search emerges clearly from letters quoted by Arthur Swinson in his biography of Sander. In December 1881, one of Sander's hunters, William Arnold, found a *Cattleya* in Venezuela that he thought might be C. *labiata vera*. 'Keep your gob shut,' Sander wrote to him, '1,000 plants would be worth £10,000 if they arrive and are genuine. A fortune! But silence . . . I am extremely excited about all this and the battle with White [a rival orchid hunter], although I wish he had yellow fever! I know you won't be outdone by him.' In the event the long-suffering Arnold wasn't outdone; he managed to ship a thousand plants to Sander, whose delight was constrained only by the poor condition in which they arrived. 'The whole world's mad on *Cattleya* at the moment,' he wrote, 'MOUTH SHUT!' Then the anticlimax: word came from the distinguished expert Professor Heinrich Gottlieb Reichenbach, to whom Sander had submitted sample for analysis, that the *Cattleya* wasn't *vera* after all, but a new variety.

Nevertheless, it was Sander who finally reintroduced the 'true' *Cattleya*. Its native home was found to be the rainforests of

Pernambuco, a thousand miles or so away from Rio. But if the place is indisputable, the circumstances of the plant's rediscovery are murky indeed, encrusted with tall stories and legend. One pleasant version has an orchid fancier spotting it in the corsage of a lady at an embassy ball in Paris, and tracking it to its source. A marginally more plausible account has Sander seeing the plant in a naturalist's greenhouse in Paris, asking where it came from, and then sending one of his collectors to the spot (possibly the unfortunate Arnold, who later disappeared up the Orinoco). Whatever the truth of the matter, by the end of 1893 Sander had plenty of *Cattleya labiata vera* to sell, and no incentive at all to provide details about where they had come from.

Almost overnight, the rare *Cattleya* became commonplace. Relatively simple to cultivate and decadently gorgeous, it quickly caught the fancy of elegant women in Paris and London. Readers of Proust will remember how in *Swann's Way* the *Cattleya* was not only the fascinating Odette's favourite flower; it had a private meaning for the lovers in the phrase 'do a cattleya', referring to what ensued when Swann undertook to arrange her corsage.

Today *C. labiata* may be the best-known of all tropical orchids, so much so that some writers betray a slight irritation in talking about it. 'The only orchid with which the average layman is at all familiar,' grumbles one, rapidly going on to speak of more interesting species. 'Plentiful today – too much so, the cut flower growers say,' complains another. Tell that to poor Arnold, sixty feet up a tree in Pernambuco.

An American Tree in London

UNTIL EIGHTY OR NINETY YEARS AGO, a huge old black walnut tree stood on the lawn of the Bishop of London's palace in Fulham, once a village on the banks of the Thames, now swallowed up in urban sprawl. In its dying days the tree looked pretty shattered: the main trunk had been struck by lightning and an 1894 photograph showed only a few leafy tufts clinging to the topmost branches, giving it the appearance of a carelessly-decorated stump. In fact, except for its size, there was nothing handsome or memorable about it. But this was a tree with a history. It had been growing there on the lawn for more than 200 years, ever since arriving, as a walnut or a young sapling, from Virginia.

These days Fulham is an unexciting residential area, closely built up with rows of terraced houses. It has a few good restaurants, plenty of petrol stations, and a lot of rush-hour traffic jams. The Bishop's palace, however, still exists in much of its ancient tranquillity, and so does its park, now covering thirteen acres out of the original thirty-six. For anyone interested in the history of gardening, and especially in the extraordinary way foreign plants have found their way into the gardens of Europe, this ought to be a hallowed spot.

You have to reach a long way back to locate the earliest gardener bishop of Fulham Palace, partly because the episcopal title to the land is itself so ancient – the oldest of any in Britain. Perhaps the first was a reverend gentleman named Edmund Grindal, who in the middle of the sixteenth century had a famous vineyard there. (He once made the mistake of sending a present of grapes to Queen Elizabeth just after one of his servants had died; gossip said that the servant had died of plague and that Grindal's grapes could have infected the Queen. He was forced to apologize, explaining that the servant had merely expired of a bad cold.) The Bishop was apparently also a connoisseur of rare plants, and is credited with importing the first tamarisk in the country, from

Switzerland, for his herb garden. Horticulturally speaking, this may have been a modest achievement, but the feathery-leafed shrub now grows wild in coastal areas around southern England.

It was Henry Compton, Lord Bishop of London from 1675 to 1713, who brought real horticultural fame to Fulham Palace. A staunch Protestant (his differences with Catholic James II temporarily cost him his job, though not his occupancy of the palace), Compton was an army officer until he was thirty. But the wealth of his family and the range of his connections – more like those of a Renaissance cardinal than an English clergyman – meant that he was bound to be a high-flyer once he decided to take holy orders. What is less obvious is why and how he became so devoted to gardening, to rare plants, and especially to trees.

The seventeenth century had already experienced the first enthusiastic stages of a boom in plant collecting. Not long before, the two John Tradescants, father and son, had put together a famous garden a few miles away in Lambeth, stocked with rarities brought back from abroad by friendly merchants and sea-captains. Interest in botany was taken for granted among such intellectuals and scientists as John Evelyn and Isaac Newton; it was linked not only with intense curiosity about the laws and functioning of the natural world, but also with theology, with plants regarded as a manifestation of God's grace. To be a plantsman was entirely consistent with being a churchman.

Perhaps this had something to do with Bishop Compton's obsession. In any case, he was in an excellent position to indulge it. The Anglican Church in the American colonies fell under the jurisdiction of the Bishop of London, and Compton was thus responsible for sending young clergymen to the New World. One of his choices was a recent Oxford graduate named John Banister (or Bannister), who may well have endeared himself to the bishop as much by his command of botanical minutiae as his familiarity with the Pentateuch. So taken by plants was Banister, in fact, that when he finally reached Virginia in 1678 – after travels in Brazil and elsewhere in South America – he set about assembling a complete natural history of the region.

With Banister in place, Bishop Compton now had a splendid source for his first love, American plants. He had already raised dozens of unfamiliar species from elsewhere in the world, among them such key introductions as the South African geranium *Pelargonium inquinans* that would later serve as one parent of the universal flowerpot geranium. Banister sent him many more. Soon his beds and hothouses were stocked with such American rarities as Indian physic (*Gillenia trifoliata*), Trillium sessile, bird violet (*Viola pedata*), Dutchman's breeches (*Dicentra cucullaria*) and, no doubt, the climber Banister had found in Brazil – *Banisteria argyrophylla*, which would bear its founder's name.

Even more notably, Banister sent trees. Some of them had been grown in England before, but never widely, and Compton's collection rapidly became famous. Studding the broad palace lawns were such hitherto unknown American species as the box elder (*Acer negundo*), swamp honeysuckle (*Rhododendron viscosum*), sweet gum (*Liquidambar styriciflua*), and sweet bay (*Magnolia virginiana*), the first magnolia to be raised in Europe. Beyond these, the Bishop also planted tulip trees, hickory, sassafras, and horse chestnuts, as well as various *Cornus* and *Crataegus*, most of them revelations to English silviculturists. In all, Compton is credited with introducing more than forty plants to Britain – with a little help from Banister and his other priestly plant hunters, of course*.

The Bishop's rarities did not remain rare for long. Even before his death in 1713, several London nurserymen were importing their own specimens. Since Compton's successor had, as one historian puts it, 'no taste for the science of Botany' and sold off everything that could be transplanted, the exotics moved quickly into the trade. Christopher Gray, whose nursery was just down the lane from the palace in Fulham, and the great Brompton Park nursery of George London and Henry Wise, eagerly augmented their stock with the Bishop's treasures, and saw to it that country

---

* Poor Banister met his end while exploring for plants along the Roanoke River in Virginia, at the age of only forty-two. He either fell from a cliff 'while,' according to one writer, 'fingering small plants from crevices', or – more probably – was accidentally shot and killed. His natural history was never finished, but the botanist John Ray published some of his drawings and descriptions of American plants.

houses across the land might boast their own examples.

Yet even Compton's plant-hating successor could not get rid of everything. Several dozen large trees survived, and apparently continued to grow peacefully as the Lord Bishops followed one another through the centuries. Among them was an American black walnut – *Nux Juglans Virginiana Nigra*, according to a list compiled by John Ray in 1687, during Bishop Compton's heyday. John Banister had probably sent it from Virginia, where it is native (Britain had only regular walnuts, *Juglans regia*, reputedly introduced by the Romans), and by 1713 it was clearly too big to transplant.

In 1751, a 'well-known botanist and electrician' named Sir William Watson visited the Fulham Palace grounds to see what, if anything, was left of Compton's garden. He found nearly forty 'exotic trees', many of them extremely large, and particularly recommended to the curious observer 'the black Virginian walnut-tree'.

Forty years later, in 1793, the number of survivors was down to twelve or thirteen – but the walnut lived on. By now it was 70 feet high, with a girth of eleven feet two inches, 'a most magnificent tree'. A hurricane in 1807 felled several of its fellows but left the walnut grand and undamaged, as an 1834 picture shows; by 1865, with the two hundred-year mark approaching, it was one of six original trees still standing. Its girth was by now 15 feet 5 inches. On 14 October 1881, a large part of it was blown down in a storm, but in 1894 enough remained to be photographed and measured – girth 17 feet 3 inches. A year or two later it was struck by lightning, but did not fall down. Someone offered £300 for the timber, an offer that wasn't accepted.

Records now become murky, but it is likely that Bishop Compton's trees were all firewood by the 1920s. Whether the last one of all was the cork oak (*Quercus suber*), the tulip tree (*Liriodendron tulipifera*), or our friend the black walnut, no one today can say. What is certain is that trees seem to have longer memories than humans do – even an American tree far from home.

Nettles

'LONG LIVE THE WEEDS,' wrote the poet Gerard Manley Hopkins, whose romantic nature led him up more than one leafy blind alley. Possibly he had dandelions or corn poppies in mind, maybe – at a stretch – a thistle. But one thing's certain: he must have overlooked *Urtica dioica*, better known as the stinging nettle.

According to the books, stinging nettles are common in the United States, having been imported (presumably accidentally) by early settlers, but I can honestly say that I never ran across them in any memorable way until I moved here. In the Berkshires, nettles weren't much of a menace, especially compared to poison ivy. They meant so little, in fact, that when I spotted my first large patch bordering a path on the edge of our woods in Skenfrith, I wasn't sure what they were. I very quickly found out.

My wife Carol is convinced that my remarkable susceptibility to nettle stings is due to the fact that I didn't grow up with them as she did in Ireland. She's practically immune, whereas if I merely brush against a nettle leaf I can still feel the painful prickles twelve or fifteen hours later. Careless weeding without gloves can have serious consequences, while any larger endeavours involving nettles require as much forethought as a sally into a bank of wild roses. I have even succeeded in getting my forehead nettled, which you have to admit takes some doing. (I was crawling under a barbed wire fence with a fly-rod at the time.)

According to *The Flora of Monmouthshire*, a fascinating compilation largely composed of records made by local amateurs with a taste for botany, the normal habitat for stinging nettles in our part of the country is 'roadsides, hedgerows, wood borders and waste places', in other words: everywhere. They are 'very common in all districts'. This is nothing more than the truth. Nettles are unavoidable.

One problem seems to be that they have no competent antagonists.

Most animals won't eat them, for obvious reasons (though my farmer neighbour claims that sheep will eat them after they're cut), and apart from the caterpillars of a few kinds of butterfly (the comma is one), insects don't pay much attention to them either. Normal plants, needing insect contact to pollinate them, might find this lack of interest awkward, but not nettles: they boast an ingenious self-pollinating system involving spring-loaded anthers that simply toss the pollen into the air, whereupon the wind carries it where nature intends it to go. It is said that on a calm morning you can sometimes see nettle pollen puffing out like tiny fountains.

There was a time when mankind regarded nettles more positively than we (or at least I) are inclined to do today. Fibres from the lanky stems were twisted into rope and woven into cloth, especially in Northern Europe, until surprisingly recently; before World War I the Germans were harvesting up to 60,000 tons of nettles a year to make soldiers' uniforms. (If this sounds penitential, it isn't: boiling renders the nettle stingless.) Some American Indians did the same. In the early 1940s, as part of the war effort, County Herb Committees in England called for 100 tons of nettles to be gathered. Mystified local collectors obliged, discovering only later that the leaves would be used for green camouflage dyes and chlorophyll extracts.

Such practical activities don't appear to have made much impact on the nettle population, nor did the ancient use of nettles for food. Nettle soup, which calls for the earliest tender tops of the plants to be plucked and boiled in stock or other liquid, has always had a following. In Ireland during the Potato Famine, starving peasants scoured the fields and ditches for nettles to eat, while in happier circumstances the Scots savoured nettle pudding: nettle tops, leeks, onions, oats, and Brussels sprouts, served with butter or gravy. (Sounds like you could leave out the nettles.) When the diarist Samuel Pepys stopped in to see his friend William Symons one cold winter day in 1661, Symons' wife thoughtfully served him a dish of freshly-made 'nettle porridge', which Pepys – who fancied himself a connoisseur – thought 'very good'.

Books of plant lore are full of received wisdom about the medical virtues of nettles. The doctrine of plant 'signatures' – which held that every plant had some human use, and that its shape, colour or other characteristic would tell you what that use was – suggested that nettles were just the thing for skin ailments, and probably wouldn't do rheumatism any harm. The treatment was flogging with a bunch of nettles. (There is a doubtful theory that the plants came to Britain in the first place with Roman soldiers who lashed themselves with nettles for warmth during the un-Italian weather.) Nettle seeds mixed with wine (how much wine?) were supposed to treat impotence, and nettle ale was taken to be a cure for jaundice. A gypsy prescription even employed nettles as a contraceptive. The man was supposed to line his socks with nettle leaves and wear them for twenty-four hours before engaging in sex. If this worked, it may have been for the wrong reasons.

On the whole, though, nettles have never had a very good press. 'What could be more odious than nettles?' asked the Roman naturalist Pliny the Elder, hardly expecting an answer, and anybody who has suffered a good stinging would heartily agree. Actually, the mechanics of the nettle sting are fascinating, and a good deal more complicated than you might think.

A nettle leaf and stem are covered with microscopic stiff hairs that can puncture skin at a touch. Until recently they were thought to do their painful dirty work by injecting formic acid (the same stuff that red ants and bees employ), but research has now revealed that a multiple whammy of at least three chemicals is involved – a histamine to irritate the skin, acetylcholine to bring on a burning sensation, and hydroxytryptamine to encourage the other two. Both of the latter, incidentally, are nerve transmitter hormones also found in animals, which – as Paul Simons points out in *The Action Plant* – raises some curious questions about the boundaries between animal and vegetable.

Various folk remedies for soothing nettle stings exist, but so far I have not found one that works for me. The classic is probably juice from a dock leaf, for which Simons offers a bit of scientific evidence: dock apparently contains chemicals that inhibit the action of hydroxytryptamine. I've tried this (it's unfortunately as easy to find a dock as a nettle around my garden), and Carol swears by it (it works in Ireland), but I just remained in pain. Another putative remedy I've read about is the juice of jewelweed. I haven't seen a jewelweed since I left New England, however, though there are supposed to be a few around. Possibly another *Impatiens*, say a nice *I. niamniamensis* 'Congo Cockatoo' – might do just as well. The most radical proposal, which comes from a book called *A Modern Herbal*, suggests applying nettle juice to the nettle sting. This 'affords instant relief'. By the time you got the juice, you'd need it.

There seems to be a belief that approaching a nettle in a calm and fearless manner, as if it were an unfriendly dog, can save you from the prickles. 'He which toucheth a nettle tenderly is soonest stung,' observed John Lyly 400 years ago, while another rhyme concludes: 'Grasp it like a man of mettle, And it soft as silk remains.' I shall leave the proof of this to others more leather-skinned, or less susceptible, than I. After all, these things demand prudence. A keeper at the Natural History Museum in London is supposed to have been stung by a nettle that had been pressed and mounted by Linnaeus two centuries before.

At Towerhill Cottage, where we live, forests of nettles are flourishing around the edges of the meadow and in the wood, particularly along the route of an old overgrown track that used to carry wagon traffic up to Coedangred Common. This is only to be expected; nettles demand phosphates, and phosphates accumulate in the soil where humans and animals deposit them over a long period of time – in gardens and churchyards, along roads, in places where creatures have lived and (especially) died and been buried. So in a way nettles are more domesticated than most wild plants, and bound to be our companions whether we like it or not. They make terrific compost, and nothing is better than an old nettlebed as a place to put a new raspberry patch.

Nevertheless, I've still got a lot of nettles that I'd like to get rid of. Back in 1878, a gentleman wrote a plaintive note to *The Garden* explaining that he had a vast patch of nettles growing under trees on his property and asked for suggestions about eradicating them. One respondent argued that if you mowed them to the ground five or six times during the growing season, 'this wears them out'. Another claimed that all you needed to do was to cut them down and dig over them shallowly. But why worry? 'All who have plenty of luxuriant nettles may rest satisfied that they have some good land.' This observation must have been of cold comfort to the nettle-beset fellow.

It was left to the well-known Victorian gardener the Reverend

Charles Wolley-Dod to come up with a really constructive solution. He had plenty of nettles, growing so vigorously that 'we have sometimes made walking sticks of them'. Wolley-Dod's solution was to plant an interesting new *Polygonum* in the midst of the nettles, thus overpowering them. It was called, he thought, *Polygonum sieboldii* (though he bought it under the name of *P. japonicum*) and he reported it 'rejoicing in the cool, damp, open soil in which nettles generally grow'. Facing up to the native inhabitants, 'it quite holds its own, and gradually beats them. It grows seven or eight feet high. . . .'

Now *Polygonum seiboldii*, otherwise known as *P. cuspidatum* (or, more recently, *Fallopia japonica*) is none other than the noted aggressor Japanese knotweed, which – we now know – spreads like wildfire and is almost impossible to eradicate. Poor Wolley-Dod. There is an old saw: 'Better stung by a nettle than prickt by a rose.' Or strangled by a knotweed, I'd say.

The Peripatetic Peony

THE BIG RED PEONIES are collapsing. They've had their day in the sun, or rather rain. A week of intermittent heavy showers has left shattered heaps of petals sticking wetly to the stone wall at the edge of the perennial bed, and only a few of the massive blooms are still able to hold their heads up. In a few days we must go round with the clippers and finish the job. Peonies, as the expression goes, are generous. It may be that they are overgenerous, considering the spectacular and wholly impractical size of their blossoms. They actually seem to be trying to please us, rather than the bees; once those chunky buds have broken, a good cloudburst is all it takes to bring on floral disaster.

No peony (no double peony anyway) is completely immune to this dire scenario, but I am talking here about the most common kind of *Paeonia officinalis*, the sort you find growing everywhere in old cottage gardens in England. In America, it is the familiar crimson 'Memorial Day peony', often appearing less luridly as pink. When we arrived at Towerhill Cottage, there was a healthy clump among the weeds; we have since split it up and replanted it in various places, with no apparent diminution in its vigor, though it took a year or two to start flowering again in a new spot. In fact, I question whether you can kill the thing – six or eight leftover roots abandoned in a bucket even started to grow without soil before I put them out of their misery.

There is, of course, a lot more to peonies than these big red ones, pleasant and appropriate as they are. Even as the scarlet monsters are disintegrating, I'm waiting to see what will happen to another more precious specimen I've got growing in our garden. At the moment it has two buds – only one of them of a size likely to bloom – and instead of the lush coarse foliage of *P. officinalis*, a rather delicate collection of stalks and very deeply-cut leaves. This is a peony with a history. I planted it last October, in the latest chapter of its extraordinary life.

My acquaintance with this particular peony began twenty-five years ago, when I bought a house in Western Massachusetts from a New York attorney named Frank Adams. Frank (or his wife – I was never quite sure) was a good gardener, judging from the plantings he entrusted to us along with the keys to the house. Some of them (such as a twisted and clearly aged quince) had been there a long time, but others had been more recently placed with an eye to effect and horticultural suitability. The peony was growing at the front of a small bed above a dry-stone retaining wall, in a spot that was obviously well-drained and enriched with manure.

One autumn day not long after we moved in, Frank came by to take away the peony. He had, I admit, warned me; that was a very special plant. Many years before, he explained, one of his wife's forebears had brought it over from England and installed it in the family garden near Boston. It flourished there, much admired. But as time passes gardens – and gardeners – change. When in the 1950s Frank bought the house in the Berkshires, he made a point of rescuing the peony and bringing it west. Now he was moving again, down into Connecticut, and felt that he should take the peony along with him. It was, after all, a rare and extremely beautiful variety, and wonderfully fragrant.

By this time I had seen the peony in bloom, and fully agreed with Adams's opinion of it. I was distressed to think of losing it. Being a nice man, Adams agreed to leave a few bits behind. I carefully dug them up and replanted them, at precisely the right depth, at several spots in the now-empty bed. In the spring spindly green shoots emerged, gradually bulked up, and before long the display was as glorious as ever. For the next fifteen years the peony went from strength to splendid strength.

In 1985 I moved to England. For various reasons, I had no opportunity to bring the peony. I often thought of it, though, and occasionally contemplated trying to identify it, so as to buy one here. At the Chelsea Flower Show one year, I went so far as to hunt through a display of blooms in search of a variety like it. No luck; it was plainly too rare and unusual. My only hope, I thought, was somehow to get a piece of rootstock from the bed in the Berkshires, and bring it back with me to England.

Finally, last autumn I got the chance I'd been waiting for. On a sunny Sunday, visiting Alford for the first time in ten years, I dug up a good-sized piece of root with four or five eyes on it, convinced my brother-in-law to shake it in a bag with some powdered sulphur to sterilize it, wrapped it in a couple of layers of plastic, and sank it deep in my suitcase, between the socks and the underpants.

In principle, smuggling plants is a lousy idea. I'll readily grant you that, even in the abstract. Eleanor Perenyi, in her delightful book *Green Thoughts*, describes how she managed to smuggle a couple of pounds of French 'Jaune d'Hollande' seed potatoes into the United States by mailing them to herself in a shoebox marked 'shoes', and apparently got away with it. But after her account was reprinted in a magazine, so I'm told, the law descended. Ms Perenyi found her vegetable garden placed under strict quarantine for two years. I suppose the same thing might – unfairly – happen to my peony.

Yet as I pushed my trolley unchallenged through customs at Heathrow with the peony root stashed among the socks, I felt nothing but satisfaction. My enterprise was restoring an unusual plant to its native place, and moreover adding to its improbable story. Think of it! Britain to Boston to the Berkshires to Britain! If I got it to grow, the circle would be closed. I would have both a rare peony and a sentimental reminder of New England.

Moreover, once the peony bloomed I'd be able to identify it. Some book, some expert would be able to tell me. It would be exciting to know just how rare it was. I could remember a lot about it – its wonderful scent, its brilliant colouring, the size and abundance of its blossoms. But identification is a tricky business and even an expert was likely to insist on seeing the real thing.

Well, I was wrong. A few weeks ago, long before the peony was due to bloom (if indeed it ever does), we spotted a garden in 'The Yellow Book' that sounded, in the circumstances, well worth going to visit. Green Cottage, in Lydney, advertised itself as having 'many herbaceous peonies, including the National Reference Collection of pre- and early post-1900 cultivars'. I had decided that peonies were something worth knowing more about. You can only learn so much from books, although I had already learned that if you count the number of buds on your peony, and come out with an odd number, someone is going to die. A slightly more dependable source informed me that the first peony to appear in England came from the Eastern Mediterranean, possibly Crete, about 1548 and was a red single. (The classic double crimson *P. officinalis* turned up in Antwerp as a chance mutation soon after.) John Gerard, the sixteenth-century plantsman who was a good gardener but a plagiarist, planted peony seeds surreptitiously so that he could claim (unsuccessfully, I gather) to have discovered a new English wildflower.

Though it had been an early spring, the peonies at Green Cottage (except for a few *officinalis*) were not yet in bloom the day we arrived. One large bed contained the National Collection, the plants growing in rows like so many vegetables, with stakes and stretched wires to keep them from falling over. Their names sounded like a guest list from Proust – 'Duchesse de Nemours', 'Général MacMahon', 'Félix Crousse', 'Madame Calot', 'Monsieur Martin Cahazac', 'Inspecteur Lavergne'. But there was no way even to guess what they would look like when the buds opened. If I was going to find my peony here, I'd have to come back a few weeks later.

As we were leaving we encountered Mrs Baber, who was tending a small collection of plants for sale in her garage. No peonies seemed to be on offer, but when she noticed us eyeing some potted specimens beneath a wire netting nearby, she asked if we had come a long way, and wanted peonies. We assured her that we were simply browsing (buying unneeded plants is all too easy) and got talking about her great love and how she sometimes imports rare specimens from a breeder in Washington State. This discussion led naturally to my telling her about my precious peony and its adventures.

What did it look like? she asked. I described what I remembered of its huge white blossoms, the flecks of scarlet, the amazing perfume, its obvious rarity. Mrs. Baber smiled. Was it a true bright 'ice' white, not cream? Were the flecks of red at random, sometimes deep among the petals? I agreed that they were. 'Festiva Maxima!' she said firmly. 'No doubt about it. It can't be anything else.'

So much for rarity. Far from being unusual, Mrs Baber explained, 'Festiva Maxima' is one of the most common peony cultivars, and has been since it was bred in France in 1851. Whole fields of them are grown in the Channel Islands for cutting and export to florists' shops. Dozens of nurseries carry them in this country; checking an American catalogue (from Gilbert Wild and Son in Missouri), I see 'Festiva' described as 'the old reliable white . . . one of the most generally planted peonies in cultivation'.

I'm not too unhappy about this. Even Mrs Baber, whose taste in peonies is about as refined as you can get, admits that 'Festiva Maxima' is a wonderful plant, scarcely bettered, and well worth growing even if the whole neighbourhood is growing the same thing. I trust it will thrive at Towerhill Cottage. In the meantime, I have developed a strong interest in peonies, and intend to try some more. They needn't be rare, by the way.

The Great White Cherry

Those weeping cherries just beyond the gallery to the left as one steps inside the gate and faces the main hall – those cherries said to be famous even abroad – how would they be this year? Was it perhaps already too late? Always they stepped through the gallery with a strange rising of the heart, but the five of them cried out as one when they saw that cloud of pink spread across the late afternoon sky.

The Makioka Sisters by Tanizaki Junichiro

A s far as the Japanese are concerned, the cherry is the essential flowering tree. Apricots, plums, peaches and pears have their place and their particular charms, but the ornamental cherry has for centuries represented not only beauty but a sort of philosophical statement about the way beauty – and life itself – can vanish in an instant, in a sudden fall of petals. Even in the midst of modern Tokyo's urban insanity (and few cities in the world can be as hectic) there are precious tracts of parkland where each spring cherries bloom and at least some contemplative souls still gather to gaze at them, sipping sake and enjoying melancholy. This in spite of the destruction wrought by war and industrialization, and Tokyo's urge to build and rebuild, generally tastelessly.

It may be that gin produces an effect different from that of sake, but cherry-blossom viewing has never caught on in the West, despite the fact that in 1912 the mayor of Tokyo presented Washington D.C. with 800 specimen Yoshino cherries (*Prunus yedoensis*). Planted in the Tidal Basin, they now yield a vast display of pinkish-white flowers on near-bare boughs each April, an attraction to tourists. But if poetry beneath the petals remains a Japanese pastime, what has caught on abroad are the trees themselves. They represent an extraordinary range of forms and colours, and flowering dates from high summer to the depths of winter. And most of the cultivated varieties (as opposed to the wild species from continental Asia and elsewhere) originated, appropriately enough, in Japan.

Probably no single person in modern times did more to encourage the spread of ornamental cherries than a wealthy, extremely long-lived plant hunter, gardener, hybridizer, and writer named Collingwood Ingram, better-known as 'Cherry' Ingram. Born in 1880, he was still gardening nearly a hundred years later in his six gloriously planted acres at Benenden in Kent. He began creating a garden there in 1919, after emerging from World War I as a captain in the RAF.

Ingram had started by studying and writing about birds, but gave it up when he decided that 'there were more ornithologists than birds'. Money was never a problem for him – the family fortune, not seriously compromised by taxes in those spacious days, came from newspapers and property – so he had plenty of opportunities for travel. He had already been to Japan in 1902 and again in 1907 searching for birds, and had been struck by the beauty of the cherries he saw there. Most were little known in the West. He decided to become an expert on them – not as a botanist in a herbarium, but as a collector and horticulturist working with the living trees.

The fact is that Ingram was hardly equipped to be an academic specialist. Suffering bad health as a child ('a herring-gutted asthmatic weakling', as he put it) he never went to school or college and was educated by tutors. When he turned to from birds to plants, he had to teach himself botany from books. But he learned well, and soon fell into the habit of going off every summer to some remote corner of the world in search of rare plants – especially rhododendrons and cistuses, as well, of course, as cherries. Eventually, he was responsible for introducing many new garden species, along with a host of splendid crosses.

Ingram had some views on collecting techniques that would certainly be frowned upon today. As he never had time to wait for his discoveries to set seed, he made a habit of digging up bulbs or seedlings in the wild and carrying them back to be raised in Kent. He worked out ways of keeping them alive – his favourite for small seedlings was a large screw-top jar ('preferably one with a mouth big enough to readily admit one's hand') half filled with damp coarse sand and a bit of charcoal – but he was the first to admit such tactics didn't always work, and even the healthiest rarities often failed to thrive in England's cool wet climate. His conscience seems to have bothered him a bit about this; at the same time as he was himself happy to scavenge for living samples, he admitted that taking 'more than an odd specimen or two' of really rare varieties unsuited to the home climate would be 'wanton vandalism'.

Cherries. of course, did not as a rule require collecting in the wild, particularly the garden varieties or 'Sato Zakura' bred over the course of centuries by Japanese horticulturists. In the 1920s Ingram began planting as many kinds of cherries as he could find, bringing some back from Japan and scrounging others, including wild species, from nurserymen and friends. Originally, as he notes in his classic 1948 book *Ornamental Cherries*, the number of Sato Zakura grown the West was no more than twenty or so, and most of those mislabelled; twenty-five years later he was able to catalogue and describe no less than fifty-one Japanese garden varieties and nearly seventy wild species from all around the world. Forty or fifty of them had never been seen in England before. Moreover, cherries had by then become everybody's favourite flowering tree – not just among blossom viewers in Ueno Park, but in gardens from Seattle to Saragossa.

Ingram lived to be 100 years old, sharp-tongued to the end (one obituarist observed that the 'vigorous and dogmatic expression of his individualist opinions . . . had not endeared him to all'). He was fond of saying that the sad thing about cherries was their tendency to die young – at only forty or fifty. (In fact, planted in partial shade so they don't exhaust themselves with flowering, some cherries can live a lot longer. Ingram describes seeing several *Prunus subhirtella* in northern Japan that were over 250 years old.) He was often asked which cherry he regarded as the best, given the huge number that had become available. His list always started with the same one: *Prunus serrulata* 'Tai Haku', meaning 'Great White' in Japanese. 'Tai Haku' is indeed a spectacular cherry. Its brilliant white single blossoms can be close to three inches across, while its young foliage is rich copper-red. Had it not been for Ingram, however, Tai Haku would be only a memory.

The story, as Ingram enjoyed telling it, goes like this. In the early 1920s an elderly lady named Freeman invited him to visit her Sussex garden. She had been an assiduous collector of rare plants in her younger days. During a trip to Provence in 1899 she had met a Frenchman who spoke in such glowing terms about some Sato Zakura he had seen in Japan that she decided then and there that she must have them. The Frenchman gave her the name of a contact in Japan, she wrote off to him, and a year later a small selection of trees arrived in England. Among them were several varieties hitherto unknown in the West. When he paid his call in 1923, Ingram found the old lady's garden to be completely overgrown. He was fascinated to hear about the cherries, however, and especially to find one survivor of the shipment in a shrubbery 'where it was being slowly but surely strangled to death by its more robust neighbours'. Although the tree was nearly dead, the sight of it electrified him. One or two branches had snow-white blossoms of a size and beauty he had never seen before, even in Japan. He prevailed upon the lady to let him come back to take a few twigs of bud-wood for propagating.

It was fortunate that he did so. A couple of years later, on another trip to Japan, he was introduced to a Mr Funatsu, described as the greatest living authority on Sato Zakura. Funatsu San had assembled a large collection of prints and drawings of cherries, and after showing them to Ingram unrolled an old *kakemono* (hanging scroll) painted by his great-grandfather 130 years before. On it, a startled Ingram saw the unmistakable likeness of his 'Tai Haku'. 'Please ask him what it is,' he said to the interpreter, and back the answer came: 'Mr Funatsu says it is a cherry that used to cultivated in the Kyoto district. It is now lost. He has been looking for it all his life without success.' The moment must have been one to prize, at least for Ingram. 'Please be good enough to tell him that I have that cherry growing in my garden in England.' Funatsu San's response was not recorded.

So every 'Tai Haku' in the world – and there are hundreds of thousands by now – is descended from Cherry Ingram's cutting, a fact which might or might not appeal to the opinionated gentleman. 'No old hand,' he once wrote, 'wants to possess a tree or shrub, however ornamental it may be, if it is planted *ad nauseam* in almost every suburban garden.' We can only hope he would make an exception for what he called 'by far the most beautiful of all the white cherries'.

The Meadow Garden

A T THE MOMENT, I'm not particularly looking forward to dealing with my flowery meadow. The grasses are a good three feet high, and the cow parsley was taller until I topped it with a sickle in hopes of discouraging further seed set (cow parsley is a thug). The wildflower count is minimal now, in high summer; even the buttercups seem to have retreated. Still, we will persist. I've booked the giant rotary mower from the tool rental shop in Coleford on the hopeful assumption that it will work better than the ever-jamming sickle-bar cutter I tried last August.

To be honest, the meadow itself is still something of an experiment. It began as an oversight a couple of years ago, when I forgot to mow it until it was out of control, or at least out of the control of my own big 22-inch rotary. It was at that point that I decided to make a virtue of my failing, having been persuaded of the many joys of a wild meadow garden. These included, of course, being in fashion.

If you believe what you read in the papers over here (which have been, incidentally, chockablock with articles on the subject), a wildflower garden in grass is a new departure. Miriam Rothschild, the doyenne of the corn cockle, has even been credited with inventing it. She started one at Ashton in 1970 and 'nothing,' she says, 'has given me more pleasure than the fact that meadow gardening has caught on'. Without wishing to denigrate her influence – after all she inspired no less a gardener than Prince Charles to copy her meadow at Highgrove – it has to be said that such spangled spreads have been around a long time. The difference is that they used to just happen, without much direct help from human beings.

Until fairly recently, Britain was blessed with thousands of acres of unimproved meadows, grassland that had never been touched by a drop of pesticide or a granule of artificial fertilizer, or reseeded for a good yield of single-species hay. These meadows were rich in wildflowers, which much prefer to grow in poor soil, and don't enjoy being bullied. But since 1945, 97 per cent of such meadows have disappeared, victims (or, if you are a modern farmer, beneficiaries) of the new practices intended to increase output. The winner, botanically speaking, has been the grasses. The losers include twenty-two species of wildflowers that have actually become extinct, as well as a vast amount of rural diversity. 'The new fields,' says one despairing ecologist, 'are about as rich in wildlife as a car park.'

Nostalgia for this vanishing treasure is one impetus behind what garden writer Stephen Lacey has called 'the most innovative theme in planting design . . . since Gertrude Jekyll'. But there are doubtless other forces at work, in view of the fact that much of the most influential work in the style is being done in Germany and Holland, not countries noted for ancient meadowland. Similarly, recent American interest in creating – or recreating – prairie gardens, featuring such plants as wild hyacinth, milkweed, and goldenrod (and burning them off periodically), is unlikely to be the result of a yearning for a return to the days before the sod-busters. In both cases, the motive seems to be a new 'green' appreciation for the beauty of wild plants and for growing them in a more natural fashion.

Of course, 'growing them in a more natural fashion' is easier said than done. There's still a pecking order, even in the world of yellow rattle and wild carrot. A hundred years ago, William Robinson could nonchalantly recommend in *The Wild Garden* that 'all planting in the grass should be in natural groups or prettily fringed colonies, growing to and from as they like after planting', but anyone who has attempted making plantings in grass knows that 'grouping' is only the beginning of the battle. The real problem is preventing the plants you want from being swamped by those you don't want.

When it comes to that, there is some difference of opinion about which plants you should want, or just how wild the garden should be. In ordinary gardening (if I may so term it), suitability is usually a matter of hardiness or design effect or possibly taste. In wild gardening it seems to be a question of how far you want to go. You can put some daffodils and crocuses in your lawn and stop mowing for a while, or you can go the whole hog and cultivate nettles. Most wild gardens are somewhere in between, and the extraordinary thing is how varied, and strangely exciting and beautiful, the permutations can be.

To a greater extent than usual, the wild gardener is at the mercy of his local conditions, as a recent international symposium at Kew made clear. Attempting a prairie garden in Shropshire just isn't on. Damp and cool summers over here mean that tough American species such as rudbeckias and the like fall prey to snails and slugs, while such English delicacies as wild orchids and cowslips would simply burn up in an Illinois summer. Grasses, too, tend to be extra vigorous in the British climate, making it necessary to concentrate on clump-forming species rather than those that spread by underground runners.

Anyone foolish enough to regard wild gardening as labour-saving, particularly in the creation stage, was also roundly disabused by speakers at the Kew symposium. Initial ground preparation can be heroic – stripping off the topsoil, for a start, and possibly keeping the ground barren for a year or two, blasting unwanted survivors with weed killer whenever they have the temerity to show their heads. Only after that can seeding take place, with a carefully balanced mixture of appropriate species. Weeding is still necessary (less so if you find thistles 'dramatic', as one wild gardener defensively claimed to do), and if you want anything special you may have to insert plugs of already-started plants. Then there is the mowing and – of first importance – the raking: if neglected, the cut grass will rot down and add nutrients to the soil.

As far as I know, my small patch of meadow has never been artificially fertilized or seeded, but it is nevertheless home to some of the most powerful and aggressive grass I have ever seen. Without any doubt, the earth there is wonderfully, hopelessly, rich, and I suspect that short of bulldozing the topsoil – which is not in the picture – I can do little about it. Six or eight years ago, when I first cleared the area of a scurf of brambles and brush, almost no grass was in evidence. The first plants to emerge in the spring were forget-me-nots, which flourished prettily and with great vigour, and a few long-neglected daffodils. But as the years passed and I mowed every month or so, grass began to get the upper hand. The forget-me-nots retreated to the edge of the wood. Celandines made an early stand, then sank, while the daffodils, saved by their good timing, continued to make a show before the grass got high. But by July, most of what you saw were the plumes of rye, timothy (*Phleum pratense*) and annual meadow-grass (*Poa annua*), along with the towering white plates of burnet saxifrage (*Pimpinella saxifraga*), cow parsley (*Anthriscus sylvestris*) and hogweed. This is still the case, but there has been some improvement.

Late last summer, a friend with a meadow much bigger and more advanced than mine – he has even produced a wild gladiolus (*G. illyricus*) among other unlikely treasures – told me about a dodge he tried on the suggestion of a wild gardening neighbour. An abandoned churchyard was about to be mowed for the first time in years. He collected sackfuls of the cut hay and spread it in his own meadow for the sake of the seed. And indeed quite a few new species appeared the next year. He offered me a few shopping bags full of his own recent cutting, which I took home and scattered.

This spring, among the daffodils, we had a splendid display of lady's smock (*Cardamine pratensis*), lovely little pale lilac-to-white blossoms that kept appearing for nearly a month. Purple knapweed (*Centaurea nigra*) has emerged, and more tall meadow buttercups (*Ranunculus acris*) than ever before. Even the grass seems more graceful. To a certain (admittedly small) degree, it is already a wildflower meadow, though perhaps not one to meet with the approval of the experts at Kew.

In order to let the seeds ripen before I chop everything down, the first mowing takes place in August, with a second mowing as late as possible in the fall to leave the grass short over the winter. There doesn't seem to be much unanimity among the experts as to the correct timing here – Christopher Lloyd, for example, mows first in early July and then again twice more before winter, but he is operating on the same principle of giving annuals time to shed their seed, and making sure the turf is low for spring flowers.

The real question, and one for which I don't expect to have an answer for several years yet, is whether my meadow will achieve – on its own – an equilibrium that includes a fair number of wildflowers. I'm reluctant to tinker. After all, what's natural about a natural garden that wants more tending than a bed full of hybrid tea roses? Such balance can occur. As the garden writer Mary Keen has noted, the untended margins of small English roads and lanes often harbour wonderful collections of native plants, quite without the help of gardeners. She mentions cowslips and orchids, followed by meadow cranesbill and mullein; in our neighborhood it's the same, plus purple loosestrife, meadowsweet (*Filipendula ulmaria*), birdsfoot trefoil and hawkweed. On the other hand, she mourns the fact that her hopefully launched wild garden is at the moment a monoculture of ox-eye daisies and grass, the clustered bellflowers and lady's bedstraw she planted having vanished. Could it be that nature is telling her – and us – something?

Mistletoe

IT WOULD HAVE BEEN NICE if the whole affair had been just slightly more Christmassy. There ought to have been Yule logs and deep snow and a few escapees from Dickens, at the very least. But what we had instead was piercing damp, sullen grey skies, half an inch of sticky red mud, and a lot of serious men in soft caps and wellies carrying notebooks. More Breughel than Boz. And, of course, an entire stockyard lot full of 'wraps' (bundles) of holly and mistletoe, being drizzled on and waiting to go under the auctioneer's hammer at the Tenbury Wells Holly and Mistletoe Sale.

Mistletoe is a very odd, almost entirely useless plant. For at least nine-tenths of the year, nobody wants it, presumably including the trees it grows on as a parasite. But as Christmas approaches, mistletoe comes into its own. So one shouldn't necessarily be surprised that so much of it has fetched up here in Tenbury Wells in a yard belonging to Russell, Baldwin and Bright, usual business sheep, cattle, houses and farms. Every florist in Britain will want at least a few sprigs to sell, and Tenbury Wells, the mistletoe capital, is the place where many wholesale dealers stock up.

I came to this auction – one of three or four that are held each year in late November and early December – to meet Stanley Yapp. Yapp is, you might say, the Voice of Mistletoe. A stocky, amiable farmer living a few miles west of Tenbury, he has become quite remarkably obsessed with mistletoe. He is an expert on its rich mythology and history and has even been known to compose poetry in praise of his favorite plant. When mistletoe goes on sale in Tenbury Wells, Yapp is sure to be there. 'It's a social occasion' – but it is also clearly a time to find out just what is happening in the market.

As far as Yapp and his friends are concerned, the most threatening thing that's happening in the mistletoe market these days is the French invasion. Traditionally, English mistletoe was cut from English trees, but it is getting harder to find, and apple orchards in Normandy are full of it. French apple farmers, moreover, are apparently convinced that mistletoe harms their trees, and have no qualms about cutting it. Their only problem is selling it, because you don't *fêter Noël* with mistletoe. So the French mistletoe is packed into cabbage crates and shipped directly to English wholesalers, sometimes spending a month or two in cold store *en route*. It is not welcome at Tenbury Wells. ('We don't want it here – and the Frenchies can keep their milk, too.') I saw only half a dozen crates, and its quality was plainly lower than that of the local variety, with fewer berries and hangdog foliage that may have been affected by a spell in deep freeze. Ironically, a French truckers' strike and a fire in the Channel Tunnel reduced the amount imported this year, but it still reportedly depressed the British market price. One Conservative Member of Parliament went so far as to call for a boycott.

For at least seventy-five years, and probably much longer, English mistletoe collectors have been scavenging the old apple orchards of the Welsh Marches – Shropshire, Gloucestershire, especially Herefordshire and Worcestershire – and bringing their clumps and bundles to Tenbury Wells for auction. Traditionally, Yapp explains, most of the collectors are gypsies, 'travelling people' who make their living picking fruit and vegetables in season. For them mistletoe – less a crop than a sort of free-for-the-picking spin-off – is a nice little earner.

I had originally been referred to Yapp when I was trying to answer a *Horticulture* reader's query about propagating mistletoe. From the flood of information Yapp provided, I was able to piece together some essential facts, the main one being that human beings *can* propagate mistletoe, but a bird – the missel thrush (*Turdus miscivorus*) – does the job much better. Dining on a white berry, which is filled with a sticky paste-like substance, he wipes his beak on a branch, leaving seeds embedded in a crevice in the bark. The mistletoe then sprouts, sending rootlets into the host tree and drawing upon it for necessary mineral nutrients.

I have since learned that it is possible to 'impregnate' a tree by smearing a well-placed mistletoe berry on a branch, though I haven't tried it; the garden writer Ursula Buchan points out that the best time to do this is March or April, when the seeds are ripe, but your Christmas sprig will by then be well over the hill. According to Plantlife, a charity devoted to saving wild plants and their habitats, 'there is no guaranteed method . . . some [people] are successful, but many remain disappointed'.

With the help of birds, however, a very wide range of species is hospitable to mistletoe. The most common hosts are old apple trees, small leaf limes (*Tilia cordata*), hawthorns, poplars, false acacias (*Robinia pseudoacacia*, which Americans call black locust), field maples (*Acer campestre*), crack willows (*Salix fragilis*) and ashes, while more exotic species from cotoneasters to horse chestnuts occasionally stand in. Yet even so, some species resist, most famously the oaks.

Mistletoe in an oak tree is a rarity, so much so that the association has accumulated its own heavy load of legend and myth. Just how much of this lore is authentically ancient and how much the result of latter-day antiquarianism may be open to question. Some authorities (Yapp is one) will tell you that mistletoe found growing in an oak was so sacred to the Druids that it had to be cut with a golden knife, allowed to fall on a white cloth held by virgins, and taken away in a cart pulled by white bulls, which were then sacrificed. Pliny, the Roman natural historian, reported this first. It makes a good story, anyway, and certainly mistletoe in an oak is hard to find. I thought I saw some the other day, but it turned out to be a clump of ivy.

According to Richard Mabey in his *Flora Brittanica*, mistletoe traditions are among northern Europe's last surviving fragments of plant magic. Kissing under it is of relatively trivial significance, considering its original standing as an aphrodisiac and the source of a fertility potion. It was supposed to cure epilepsy and measles, reduce tumors and fend off witches. Farmers treated sheep and cattle with it. Yapp recalls how in the Tenbury neighborhood it was customary to take down the mistletoe after Twelfth Night, set it alight, and then run with the burning branch across the nearest field of growing grain, thereby assuring a good crop. Powerful stuff! Until recently – no more than thirty years ago – mistletoe could not even be used to decorate churches in some parishes, Mabey says, because of its pagan implications.

Just as Clement Moore and *The Night Before Christmas* probably has more to do with our modern notion of Father Christmas than any amount of ancient folklore, the association between mistletoe and Christmas is of relatively modern origin. In those parts of England and Wales where it commonly grew, local traditions usually connected it to New Year celebrations, and the period running up to Candlemas (2 February). In the eighteenth century a Reverend William Stukeley popularized Druidism as a sort of primitive Christianity, creating a fad that spread through the country; the custom of kissing under the mistletoe probably thus derives from a sanitized version of fertility rites that may never have existed. In naming his enormous treatise on primitive beliefs *The Golden Bough* (mistletoe turns golden after being hung up for a few months), Sir James Frazer didn't help matters much.

Still, if you are lucky enough to see a pale yellow-green cascade of mistletoe growing from the otherwise bare branches of an apple tree on an icy midwinter day, surrounded by a chirruping flock of birds feeding on the berries, it will be obvious why this plant came to be regarded with a certain uncomfortable respect. At a time when everything else was dead, it was alive; normal plants rooted themselves in the earth, while it seemed to live on air. I'm delighted to note that our biggest apple tree at Towerhill Cottage is now host to a small spray (still berryless – it may need a partner), and that an old orchard down in the valley near Skenfrith has half a dozen splendid clusters that the gypsies have apparently not yet spotted.

Yet there are hints that in Britain as a whole mistletoe is scarcer than it used to be, even a few years ago. While prices at Tenbury Wells did not reflect this (only 50p to 75p a pound average), serious shortages were reported in London last Christmas, and there was almost nothing left to collect in some hitherto fruitful areas. What remains is more and more found far above ground in tall trees. Attempts – doubtfully successful, as you might guess – have been made to harvest such high clumps by shotgun.

Together with the Botanical Society of the British Isles, Plantlife recently conducted a major survey of mistletoe, the first since 1970, on the plausible presumption that it may someday – if not already – be an endangered species. Calculations are not yet complete, but according to

Jonathan Briggs, who is coordinating the data, it isn't quite time for panic stations. Dots on the sightings map in mistletoe's West Country heartland seem to be further apart than they were twenty-five years ago, yet more reports could still close some of the gaps. What the preliminary findings have done, however, is to confirm distribution patterns and show that elderly full-size apple trees remain the favourite host, harbouring nearly 40 per cent of all sightings.

This ancient alliance may represent the most serious threat to mistletoe's future. All through the rolling orchard-covered hills of the Marches, aged apples are being grubbed out and replaced with smaller bush-type trees less welcoming to mistletoe and more easily harmed by it. In the end it may not be the gypsies lugging Christmas bundles to Tenbury Wells that spells oblivion for this botanical oddity in Britain, but the hybrizers, the efficiency experts, and the man who invented the mechanical apple-picker.

'The Most Interesting
Plant in North America'

IT DOESN'T SOUND LIKE MUCH, really. 'A charming, small, but not easily grown evergreen perennial for the experienced plantsman', is all that one standard handbook can manage to say on its behalf. But according to the great American botanist Asa Gray, *Shortia galacifolia* – otherwise known (if at all) as Oconee bells or little coltsfoot – was (sound of trumpets) 'perhaps the most interesting plant in North America'. What could have possessed him?

The story is a curious one, involving three continents, numerous frustrated plant hunters, and even Charles Darwin himself. It starts back in the eighteenth century with the French botanical explorer and spy André Michaux. Commissioned to scavenge the back country of the United States in search of native trees that might help restore France's dangerously depleted timber stock, Michaux travelled thousands of difficult miles between 1785 and 1792 collecting plants. In all, he rode, walked or paddled through three-quarters of the states or territories east of the Mississippi (to say nothing of excursions to Quebec and the Bahamas), suffering hardships that can only be guessed at from the laconic entries in his surviving journals. His most frequent complaint, in fact, is that his horses keep straying at night and take hours to find again.

Michaux's favourite collecting area was the Carolinas and Georgia, partly because from 1786 on he made Charleston, South Carolina his base. Again and again he trekked northwards across the Carolina Piedmont to scour the high mountains east of what is now Asheville, North Carolina – Roan Mountain, Grandfather Mountain and others. He also went into the Smokies and to the headwaters of the Savannah River. And somewhere in this country he found and preserved a specimen of a plant new to him. It was incomplete, consisting only of leaves, stem and a single fruit. Along with many other more impressive discoveries, the specimen eventually found a place in the Michaux Herbarium in the Musée d'Histoire Naturelle in Paris, identified only by a location tag reading 'Hautes montagnes de Carolinie'.

Now we move to 1839. Young Asa Gray was travelling in Europe, ostensibly buying scientific books for the fledgling University of Michigan, but in fact indulging his first love by meeting botanists and investigating herbaria. In the Michaux Herbarium he came upon the still-unclassified plant from Carolina, and realized with excitement that it actually represented a new genus. The find also suggested to him that the Carolina mountains were an area ripe for botanical exploration.

But the mysterious plant proved to be elusive. In 1841 Gray made the first of several trips into the region, despite warnings from an acquaintance that 'you will be obliged to put up with accommodations on the way, *such as you never dreamed of*' while letters of recommendation to locals wouldn't be needed, because 'I doubt if they can read'. In any case, Gray couldn't find the plant, search as he would through the rhododendron-choked valleys and along the rocky cliffs. In 1842, however, he ventured to publish, together with his colleague John Torrey, a description based on the sketchy material in Paris. Having claimed 'the right of a discoverer' to name it, he called it *Shortia galacifolia* after Dr A. W. Short, a well-known Kentucky amateur botanist, and the *Galax*-shaped leaves.

Shortia became a kind of Holy Grail for collectors. In the words of Charles Sprague Sargent (whose own involvement in the story comes a bit later) 'the keenest-eyed plant hunters looked for it in vain year after year in all the region in which Michaux was supposed to have travelled.' Not until 1877 was it found, and then in the wrong place – not the high mountains at all, but on the banks of the Catawba River near Marion, North Carolina. A teenage boy named George Hyams gave it to his father, a professed herbalist, who didn't realize what a precious thing he had for more than a year.

Gray was delighted ('Now let me sing my *nunc dimittis*,' he wrote); with complete specimens in hand he could confirm and refine his description. In 1879 he went with his wife on a pilgrimage to North Carolina so that he could see the sacred spot for himself. The fate of the Catawba *Shortia* was less happy; poachers dug up every plant they could find for sale at high prices. Attempts at garden use came to nothing and rapid extinction appeared inevitable.

But was this only place *Shortia* could be found? Gray continued to have great faith in the accuracy of Michaux. If Michaux said the plant had come from the high mountains, then that's where it came from. The Catawba specimens must be a separate group, perhaps washed down from the mountains immediately to the west. Searchers proceeded to cover these slopes with great care. Nothing. *Shortia* seemed doomed to being lost yet again.

In the autumn of 1886, Charles Sprague Sargent, founder of Harvard's Arnold Arboretum and by then America's most distinguished dendrologist, journeyed to the wild corner where Georgia, North and South Carolina come together. This mountain region, about seventy-five miles southwest of the point where George Hyams found *Shortia*, was well outside the previous search range. Sargent was trying to discover something about the origins of a magnolia whose roots Michaux had collected here in December of 1788. As it turned out, there had been a confusion of names and Sargent's magnolia venture came to nothing, but in examining Michaux's journal for the period he noticed something else. On the day the explorer arrived in the mountains – hungry and cold and suffering from high fever – he had made note of a 'Nouvel Arbuste a.f. dentelés rampant sur la Montagne' ('New shrub with denticulated [minutely notched] leaves flourishing on the mountain.') He apparently collected samples, but said no more about it.

Michaux's directions to the point where he had camped were so detailed that Sargent was able to follow them easily, and to trace the excursions the plant-hunter had made. At the junction of two 'torrents', the Toxoway and the Horse-pasture, in a 'little fertile plain', Sargent discovered *Shortia*. This was almost certainly the source of the plant in the herbarium in Paris that Gray had come upon a century before. Many more were later found in the general area (including Oconee County, South Carolina, whence its common name), although because of dam and road building, aggressive collecting, and the incursion of civilization in the form of farms and second homes, they have once again become rare in the wild.

Why Michaux called it a 'shrub' remains a mystery – *Shortia* is without question a herbaceous perennial, though no doubt it doesn't show its best face in December. But why Asa Gray termed it 'perhaps the most interesting plant in North America' is clearer. This has little to do with its beauty (modest) or its elusiveness (legendary), but rather with the role *Shortia* played in the greatest scientific drama of the nineteenth century, the debate over Charles Darwin's *Origin of Species*.

In the years before Darwin published his epochal work, Asa Gray had been one of his primary correspondents, supplying him with information and exploring aspects of plant distribution and other key subjects on which Darwin's thesis would depend. He was one of the very few people to whom Darwin revealed himself, and a man whose own adventurousness in building large ideas out of an infinity of close observations could match Darwin's own. In time, though the two of them were far too strong-minded and individual to align their opinions perfectly, Gray would become Darwin's principal American supporter and spokesman, simultaneously doing much to create a modern scientific establishment for the United States.

In 1858, Gray was examining a group of specimens from Japan brought back by Commodore Perry's expedition. For a long time – indeed from the time the first collectors had begun sending samples of Japanese species to Europe and America – botanists had been aware of an odd fact: certain plants could be found in Japan and in the eastern United States but nowhere else. With this flood of new material, the connection appeared ever stronger. Now, suddenly, Gray recognized something familiar: a plant almost identical to his own *Shortia galacifolia*. It had been resoundingly named *Schizocodon uniflorus* by a Russian botanist (in Japanese it was called 'iwa-uchiwa' or 'crag fan' from the shape of its leaves), but it was without question a *Shortia* (and would eventually go by that name too).

But how was one to account for this peculiar identity between two so widely-separated flora, marooned on opposite sides of the world? Given the still-primitive level of understanding about geological history current at the time – and his own ignorance of that branch of science – Gray's explanation of the connection was brilliant. He concluded that during the last ice age, the spread of glaciers had forced plant species common to the entire North Temperate Zone of America and Asia to retreat southwards, and only where there was room for them to shelter in agreeable surroundings just beyond the reach of the ice (as in Japan and the eastern United States) did they survive. When the glaciers melted back, changed conditions made it impossible for many species – including *Shortia* – to follow, and they were left isolated.

Gray's thesis fitted beautifully into Darwin's grander argument, and helped support it. Many plants, from pachysandra to magnolias, had been involved in illustrating the Japan–America link. But *Shortia*, still at that date blooming unseen in the Carolina mountains, already represented something special to Asa Gray. It must have fascinated him more than ever, maybe even enough to make him call it 'perhaps the most interesting plant in North America'.

Hyacinthine Dragons and Strawberry Delights

M Y SOLE VENTURE INTO THE WORLD of tree peonies so far is a large specimen called *Paeonia lutea* var. *ludlowii*. It may also be called *P. delavayi* var. *ludlowii*. It also may be plain *Paeonia lutea*. The fact is, I'm not sure. All I'm sure about is that it is a gawky shrub now about seven feet tall with rather undistinguished single yellow flowers that tend to be invisible because they hide behind the leaves. The leaves themselves are nice – deeply cut and copious, in a pleasing shade of green, and they wave gracefully when the wind blows.

I have always approached the idea of growing tree peonies with great wariness, assuming that they are tender and difficult; seeing a group of them bundled up for winter at Naumkeag in Stockbridge, Massachusetts, like so many schoolchildren getting ready for a snowball fight, made a powerful impression. One despairing English grower a century ago claimed that a tree peony died a foot for every six inches it grew. But the *Ludlowii* (let's call it that for simplicity) has given me courage. It seems perfectly happy in the climate of South Wales, so perhaps some of its more elegant relatives will be too. I'm looking into it.

In the meantime, I have to confess a long fascination with these plants, as much with their names and their extraordinary history as with their often over-the-top beauty. Peonies in general are pretty good, but tree peonies are really something special. The saga of their arrival in Western gardens and the achievement of dogged breeders in creating new cultivars can hardly be matched by any other group of species.

The story begins (and to some extent still continues) in China. For hundreds or possibly thousands of years, tree peony fanciers in the Orient have been breeding new varieties. The plants were enormously popular; particularly rare and unusual examples could bring huge prices, and in the Tang Dynasty there were even episodes of 'peonymania' like the tulipmania of the Dutch. A millenium ago the fad spread to Japan. By the time Western plant-hunters turned up, the range of cultivars was so wide and sophisticated that confusion about their parentage – about the original species tree peonies from which they must have been bred – was inevitable.

The first examples to reach Europe were, obviously, hybrid varieties picked up by merchants and visitors in eastern China and Japan. The great collector Robert Fortune, for instance, tracked down a couple of dozen kinds near Shanghai in the 1840s and succeeded in getting them back to England alive with the help of the newly-invented Wardian cases. Philipp von Siebold sent forty varieties from Japan to Holland in 1844. Tree peonies were known in Europe by the name Moutan (properly Mudan), a term used by the Chinese to refer to all peonies, tree peonies and herbaceous peonies alike. Later, the name *Paeonia suffruticosa*, meaning 'shrubby' peonies, came into use.

It soon became apparent that almost all of these first tree peonies, fashionable as they might be among rich European gardeners, were actually cultivars, not species. They would not produce dependably from seed, which meant that breeding was even worse than hit-or-miss. Before any kind of hybridization could be undertaken, what was needed was specimens of the wild species varieties.

In the 1880s the French missionary Jean Marie Delavay, working in the remote province of Yünnan in south-western China, found what appeared to be two different wild tree peonies and sent them back to Paris. One, subsequently named *P. delavayi*, had small dark red single blossoms, the other, *P. lutea*, had yellow. Neither appeared to be of much garden interest; the prominent French horticulturist Maxime Cornu went so far as to declare dismissively that *P. lutea* would never amount to anything. (Had he lived, Cornu might have regretted his words a few years later when botanist Louis Henry created a splendid *P. lutea* hybrid and, probably tongue in cheek, named it 'Souvenir de Maxime Cornu'.)

Other original species tree peonies proved harder to find, and arguments about their status continued. As early as 1802, an English sea captain had brought back from China a tree peony thought to be a species, a white semi-double with purple blotches, but it was not seen in the wild until 1914. In that year Reginald Farrer, the word-mad rock garden guru and plant collector, found it in Gansu Province ('above the sere and thorny scrub the snowy beauties poise and hover, and the breath of them went out upon the twilight as sweet as any rose'). It was another twenty years, however, before the American explorer Joseph Rock was able to collect seed of the plant, which came to be known as *P. suffruticosa* 'Rock's Variety' (or, more properly, *P. rockii*), from a monastery garden. Other candidates – *P. potanini*, *P. jishanensis*, and *P. ostii* – have since been discovered and placed in the family tree. All grow wild in China, or at least did until the demand for peony root bark in Chinese medicine led to the virtual extinction of most of them.

Juggling the taxonomy of these species has been ceaseless, with some names going (for example the useful *suffruticosa* has recently come under fire, to be replaced by *jishanensis*, *ostii*, and *rockii*) and others coming (a Chinese botanist not long ago identified a species named *P. quii*). Keeping track of all this is too much for me (and, I suspect, for some professionals). In any case, the important point is that the emergence into horticulture of these wild varieties with their steady, reproducible and rich gene pools meant that hybridization could begin seriously. It promptly did.

Hybridizing tree peonies is a slow and generally frustrating process. To secure seeds, pollen from a plant of one variety (the 'pollen parent') must be applied to the stigma of the 'pod parent' – but before this can be done, the petals and anthers of the pod parent must be carefully removed. Afterwards the blossom must be bagged to prevent stray pollen from getting in. Another complexity lies in the fact that the two varieties may bloom at different times, so the pollen might have to be dried or otherwise preserved until needed. Dozens of crosses may produce few viable seeds – or none at all. Then, from the time a seed is planted to the time a blossom appears can take ten years or more, and there's no way of telling whether the hybrid is worthwhile until you see the blossom. Many attempts, moreover, result in no improvement. Yet some do, and this is what draws the breeders on.

The seeds of *P. lutea* and *P. delavayi* that Abbé Delavay sent to Paris had no sooner begun blooming around the end of the nineteenth century than French hybridizers set out to combine the vitality of the species with the rich beauty of the imported oriental Moutans. Professor Henry, and after him the plantsman Victor Lemoine, succeeded in creating half a dozen magnificent cultivars with distinctive forms and colours (mostly yellows) that are nearly all still available commercially. The one failing of these hybrids is a tendency for the large flowers to droop, because Henry and Lemoine had been forced to use the heavy double Chinese Moutans as pod parents rather than the more upright and lighter Japanese varieties.

Lemoine continued to make more crosses, but the true focus of the hybridizing scene soon shifted to upstate New York, where A. P. Saunders, a chemistry professor at Hamilton College, began producing a long series of extraordinary tree peonies. Saunders objected to the French droopiness, and solved it by making use of single and semi-double Japanese Moutans as pod parents and pollen from both *P. lutea* and *P. delavayi*. Saunders' peonies held their heads up. They also displayed a range of colours never seen in tree peonies before, ranging from clear yellows to the near-black of the dramatic 'Black Pirate'.

Challenges remained. Attempts to make reverse crosses (pollen from the Moutan to the species) failed. More important, none of the new hybrids, either French or American, was fertile. Some produced seed, but the seed never germinated. Finally, after hundreds of trials, two seeds sprouted and grew into fertile plants. Their flowers were nothing to brag about, but they offered the possibility of yet another new departure in breeding.

In his seventies, Saunders decided to retire, having by then recorded some 15,000 hybrids of both herbaceous and tree peonies. His collections – including the two precious second-generation (F2) hybrids – went to a younger colleague, William Gratwick of Geneseo, New York, whose work in turn attracted the attention of a Greek-born New York artist named Nassos Daphnis. Each spring for more than fifty years, Daphnis travelled north to make tree peony crosses at the Gratwick nursery. The reverse cross of Moutan on species was achieved, giving rise to a famous range of cultivars including 'Boreas' and 'Hephestos'; so, after many frustrating failures, was the successful hybridization of Saunders' F2 plants, 'back-crosses' involving further generations, and still more exceptional tree peonies, some of which are not yet on the market.

Nobody has figured out a way to make the hybridization process any simpler or quicker, but since World War II many breeders in the US and abroad have been exploring new routes using different species and Moutan parents. One Japanese grower, Toichi Itoh, even managed to cross tree peonies and herbaceous peonies, thus creating what are known as Itoh hybrids or intersectionals. Poor Itoh died before seeing his plants bloom, but his success has been followed up by such American breeders as Roger Anderson and Don Hollingsworth.

So far as tree peonies are concerned, there may be a degree of poetic justice in the fact that China, their old home, has in recent years come back to centre stage. Barred for decades. foreign botanists are able to visit and get information from Chinese scientists, while the Chinese themselves have been encouraged to study and try to protect their peony heritage. Exporters are making the classic Chinese Moutan varieties increasingly available in the West.

I have only one problem with this otherwise welcome development – the names. Traditionally, Chinese cultivar names are not straightforward. Where American grower David Reath might choose to call his new hybrid 'Strawberry Delight', a Chinese grower prefers something like 'Hyacinthine Dragon Lying in an Ink Pool', or 'Smiling in the Thickets', or 'Coiled Dragon in the Mist Clutching a Purple Pearl'. Now this would be okay if there were some consistency involved, but is clear from catalogues that whoever is passing on translations (or, for that matter, the spelling of the names in Chinese romanization) has a weak grasp of one or the other of the two languages. To someone who, like me, has a smattering of Chinese, this linguistic dither is offensive. It ought to be straightened out. For a small fee – or a few tree peonies – I'd be happy to oblige.

SOME PEOPLE

Jagadis Chunder Bose

I DON'T GO OUT OF MY WAY to look for oddballs in the world of gardening, but it does seem to me sometimes that there are a lot of them about. Fanatics of one sort or another, pursuers of non-existent truths, propagandists for solely-owned theories – you can find them all. Still, one man's crank is another man's genius. I'm still not quite sure where to place Sir Jagadis Chunder Bose, and I gather I'm not alone in my indecision.

Bose – and I call him by his surname alone with some reluctance – is usually referred to as a botanist, though his real expertise lay elsewhere, in plant physiology, or physics, or possibly electrodynamics. (He also had a fair line in theosophical metaphysics, but so far as I know this did not play a major role in his scientific activities.) What he is known for, so far as he is known at all these days, are his attempts to demonstrate that plants can respond to stimuli in the same way that other living organisms, from jellyfish to humans, can – indeed (to put it crudely) that plants have feelings.

Now this may smack of that notorious volume of pseudo-science published a few years ago, *The Secret Life of Plants*, and it is certainly significant that Peter Tompkins and Christopher Bird, its authors, include in it an exhaustive (if uncritical) account of Bose's career and work. Bose was nevertheless a serious scientist. Born in what is now Bangladesh in 1858, he took his first degree at Calcutta University and then did postgraduate work in experimental physics at London University and Cambridge, mostly tinkering with the newly-discovered radio waves. Some admirers claim he could have beaten Marconi to the wireless telegraph, had he not refused to patent his own device. On one occasion in Calcutta he succeeded in transmitting a signal through three walls (and the corpulent chairman of the meeting) to set off a bell, fire a pistol, and detonate a small bomb.

In India, Bose taught and continued his experimental work. One day he noticed an odd phenomenon: a metal part in one of his radio receivers became 'tired' with use, and then slowly recovered. Pursuing this notion, Bose was soon claiming that various metals could suffer fatigue and then be restored by the metallic equivalent of gentle massage or a warm bath; you could even 'poison' a metal and then bring it back to life with an antidote. Papers presenting these findings in Paris and London were, according to his admiring biographer, 'highly appreciated'.

It was at this point that Bose began thinking about plants. If animals and metals, at the extremes of 'living' and 'non-living', could be shown to share behavioural characteristics, then what he called 'the vast expanse of the silent life of plants' ought to be explored. 'Full of this idea', he rushed out of his London lodging, collected chestnut leaves, and subjected them to his usual test involving electrical stimulation and measurement of reactions. They responded vigorously. So did the carrots and turnips he tried next, although a sample of sea-kale was inert; this mystery was solved when the greengrocer admitted that it had been snowed on. Clearly, he concluded, all matter was intimately related, 'a multiform unity in the great ocean of being'.

Bose discovered more and more similarities between the reactions of plants and animals challenged by various stimuli. He administered poisons of different kinds, showing that the curves of response in the plants were remarkably similar to that in animal muscle. He made plants 'fatigued' and measured how long and in what way they recovered. He put plants to sleep with chloroform, and woke them up again. He even managed to transplant a large pine tree under anaesthesia, claiming that it did not suffer the usual shock.

Until now Bose had been held in high, if wary, respect by the panjandrums of European science, but his reputation was due for a setback. Presenting the results of his startling findings before the august Royal Society in London in June 1901, he was attacked from an unexpected quarter. Sir John Burdon Sanderson, the foremost British expert on plant responses, had continued Darwin's researches on the physiology of the Venus's Flytrap, discovered electrical nerve-like activity in the plant, and might have been expected to be sympathetic. He was not. Bose, he declared, should not be interfering in fields where he lacked competence, such as physiology. His paper should not be published. Other senior figures concurred; the paper was relegated to the archives.

Were they fair? Probably not entirely – to some extent Sanderson was acting out of pique because he had been upstaged. Some of what Bose proposed was plainly off the wall, though not all; he had, and continued to have, such distinguished supporters as Sir Sidney Vines, then president of the Linnean Society, and the philosopher-scientist Herbert Spencer. His rhetoric did him no particular good, larded as it was with cosmic notes about 'the thrill in matter', nor did his deliberate attempt to breach the boundaries between established disciplines gain him friends. Worst of all – though no one was so rude as to say so – was the fact that he was, after all, an Indian. As one hostile animal physiologist, later a convert, told him, 'I thought your Oriental imagination had led you astray.'

Shocked and offended, Bose fought back in the laboratory, devising new experiments and producing papers at a great rate. He now concentrated on studying plant responses, employing his favourite *Mimosa pudica* (the sensitive plant, which has the happy habit of reacting instantly to being touched by drooping and folding up its leaves), along with *Desmodium gyrans,* the telegraph plant, an Indian species which moves its leaves up and down like a semaphore. His aim was to devise ways of telling how a plant felt under different conditions. How would it react to a specific stimulus if it was in an excited state? A depressed state? Dying? The trick was to invent instruments capable of registering and recording what were often extremely subtle and elusive reactions, to make plants produce (as he later put it) their 'autographs'.

In spite of trips back from Calcutta for demonstrations and lectures, Bose did not get along well with the English scientific establishment. The Linnean Society accepted a paper, but the Royal Society continued obdurate, and he eventually began publishing his own reports of his work in a long parade of diagram-filled books. *Response in the Living and the Non-Living* appeared in 1902, followed by *Plant Response as a Means of Physiological Investigation, Researches on the Irritability of Plants, Life Movements in Plants* (in three volumes), *The Nervous Mechanism of Plants, Plant Autographs and their Revelations* and more. With patience and a willingness to overlook repetition, it is possible to trace in them Bose's wonderful adventures along the border between plant and animal.

One series of experiments, for example, established that the skins of grapes, tomatoes, frogs, tortoises and lizards 'behave substantially alike', and that the digestive systems of insect-eating plants worked the same way as the stomachs of various animals. Using an array of Heath Robinson devices to magnify responses, potentially as much as one hundred million times (so he claimed), he measured the reaction of plants to irritation (being rubbed with a piece of cardboard, shocked with electricity, struck sharply), to being drugged with alcohol, chloroform and other substances (some suffered hangovers), to being heated or chilled. He produced death spasms, and discovered that when plant tissue died it produced an electric discharge. (A half-pea, he calculated, could give off as much as half a volt, so a pan of 500 pairs of half-peas, suitably hooked up in series, would be enough to electrocute the cook!) He made tendrils of climbing plants coil on demand with the help of electricity, and studied the phenomenon of memory in plants, suggesting that they could be trained to respond to particular stimuli. And while sensitive plants like the mimosa were his chosen subjects, he also worked with vegetables normally regarded as hopelessly inactive. About 1914, the magazine *Nation* ran the following tongue-in-cheek report after a visit to Bose's London laboratory:

> In a room near Maida Vale there is an unfortunate carrot strapped to the table of an unlicensed vivisector. Wires pass through two glass tubes full of a white substance; they are like two legs, whose feet are buried in the

flesh of the carrot. When the vegetable is pinched with a pair of forceps, it winces. It is so strapped that its electric shudder of pain pulls the long arm of a very delicate lever which actuates a tiny mirror. This casts a beam of light on the frieze at the other end of the room, and thus enormously exaggerates the tremor of the carrot. A pinch near the right-hand tube sends the beam seven or eight feet to the right, and a stab near the other wire sends it as far to the left. Thus can science reveal the feelings of even so stolid a vegetable as the carrot.

Bose was particularly proud of his machines, and reproduced detailed drawings in his books showing how they were constructed. One, which he called the Crescograph, was actually capable of indicating – on the spot – just how fast or slow a plant was growing, and he could use it to measure the effect of short-term factors like a flash of light. (The flash apparently jolted the plant; weak radio waves speeded growth, strong ones slowed it.) Other devices helped him explore how some plants 'sleep', exhibiting a pattern of 'awareness' and 'insensibility' through the course of the day ('*Mimosa* is a late-riser').

Bose was so convinced that plants had nerves – they certainly behaved as though they did – that he spent much time and energy trying to find one. He finally concluded that he had isolated nerve tissue in a fern stalk. The mimosa, he was sure, was likewise equipped, but the 'phloem-strand' in question couldn't be removed 'without tearing it to pieces'. As Brent Elliott notes in a recent article on Bose, 'Subsequent researchers have not been persuaded.'

Today, seventy or eighty years on, much of Bose's work has been overtaken by complexities of knowledge and information that I would hesitate to discuss even if I were able. To the extent that he was utterly convinced of his own rightness – he almost never made use of anyone else's discoveries, or built on related research, meanwhile scrupulously ignoring competing evidence – he prejudiced his case, and drifted further and further from the scientific mainstream. Yet according to a recent book by Paul Simons, *The Action Plant*, in certain important ways Bose deserves more respect than he has received. Sir Jagadis, Simons points out, 'was the first person to appreciate fully that electrical signals control leaf movements in [mimosa]', and succeeded in showing that 'plant excitability has much in common with animal nerves'. Now that's not quite as sensational as proving that your rhododendron can be as affectionate as your cat, but it sounds to me like perfectly plausible science.

Joseph Rock

AS PLANT HUNTERS GO, Joseph Rock was not a lucky man. Far from leading a charmed life, he led what can only be regarded as a frustrating one. One disaster after another attended his progress, on top of which he seems to have been notably unlikeable. The editor of *National Geographic Magazine*, who published several articles by Rock, pronounced him 'one of the most cantankerous of human beings'. He also had a bad stomach.

It is a mournful fact, typical of the way Rock played hide and seek with fame, that the most famous plant bearing his name – *Paeonia rockii* (or *P. suffruticosa* ssp. *rockii*), a rare and beautiful tree peony – was not even his own discovery, and his introduction of the seeds passed almost unnoticed*. Not for Rock the cheers that greeted E. H. Wilson's *Lilium regale* or Frank Kingdon Ward's blue poppy. Though he spent in all more than fifty years collecting plants, introducing no fewer than 493 species of rhododendron into the Western world (more than were known before, all told), as well as many kinds of *Berberis*, *Meconopsis*, *Primula* and *Potentilla*, and collected thousands of valuable herbarium specimens, poor Rock never really hit it big.

Josef Franz Karl Rock was born in Vienna in 1884, and from the first evinced interest in unusual forms of scholarship. When was ten he started to learn Arabic, and by sixteen was teaching it. Chinese came next. Bridling at family plans to make him enter the priesthood, he set off for England, but – predictably – never got there; he missed the

---

* Reginald Farrer may claim credit for first seeing it growing in the wild, in China's Kansu Province in 1914. He apparently failed to collect plants or seeds. Sometime after 1925, Rock spotted the plant in a lamasery garden at Choni in Kansu, and sent seeds back to the Arnold Arboretum. In 1928, the lamasery – and its gardens – were laid waste, but by the late Thirties the peony (by then called Paeonia suffruticosa 'Joseph Rock' or 'Rock's Variety') had been flowered in several countries.

Channel steamer at Antwerp and in a fit of enthusiasm booked passage to America instead.

Josef became Joseph. Wandering from place to place around the States in search of a climate that would favour his weak chest, Rock picked up English in Texas and eventually arrived in Hawaii, where he gained both his health and a job teaching Latin and natural history. Up to this point he had shown few signs of any interest in botany, much less expertise, but in 1908 he suddenly blossomed as the first ever Botanical Collector for the Hawaiian Division of Forestry and began churning out an amazing number of learned articles and books on everything from trees to algae. To assist in the latter study, he convinced a rich local man to build him a glass-bottomed boat. He also found time to assemble an impressive herbarium and to take up American citizenship.

Being Rock, however, problems arose. The Forestry Division ran out of funds; he shifted to the College of Hawaii, where he taught and continued to clamber through the hills collecting. He was not happy teaching; his few students remembered him as 'temperamental as a prima donna'. Moody and private, he later admitted that he was 'dreadfully lonely'. Trips at his own expense to the Far East, and once around the world, cheered him a bit, but by 1920 he was ready to quit. The last straw was a decision to move his precious herbarium – by then some 25,000 specimens – out of his control. Furious, he headed for the mainland to look for another job.

As his biographer S. B. Sutton observes, specialists in Hawaiian botany were not exactly in demand at the time. After several turndowns, however, he struck upon an opportunity that seemed likely to justify all his previously unrewarded efforts. The Office of Foreign Seed and Plant Introduction of the United States Department of Agriculture wanted someone to find the mysterious chaulmoogra tree, source of what promised to be the first effective cure for leprosy. Who better than Joseph Rock?

Though chaulmoogra nuts had appeared in Thai and Burmese markets, the tree itself (*Taraktogenos kurzii*) was elusive. Rumour placed it in the Doi Sootep Mountains west of Chiangmai, but all Rock could find were leeches and a number of gilded temples, which he photographed. Travelling first by boat and then overland through dense tropical forests ('inhabited by tigers, leopards and snakes', he noted) to Burma, he was advised by natives that the tree grew in the Kalama Range north of Moulmein. The tree in question, though a near relative, turned out to be the wrong one, so Rock pressed on. When he finally found *T. kurzii*, in jungle north of Mandalay, the first specimens were without nuts, but by scouring the countryside he at last got what he was looking for. He also got an unexpected bonus in excitement. His party was stalked by a man-eating tiger, which killed a village woman. With Rock's help the natives trapped it – using the woman's body as bait. Then, loaded with seeds of the chaulmoogra tree, Rock trekked back to civilization.

Unfortunately for him, though his adventure made good copy for *National Geographic* (once his text had been rewritten by the long-suffering editors), it soon developed that the chaumoolgra oil he had gone to so much trouble to find was not a miracle cure for leprosy after all. It worked in some cases, but the side effects were insupportable, and researchers moved on to other treatments. Poor Rock had to move on too. Still supported by the USDA, he travelled north to hunt for plants in China proper, finally settling in the town of Likiang in the western province of Yunnan where he would spend most of the rest of his life.

Here he collected in earnest – tens of thousands of plant specimens, more thousands of bird and mammal skins – and explored the mountains and valleys on the borders of Tibet. It was great country for rhododendrons and primulas, although the cream had already been skimmed by such predecessors and competitors as George Forrest, Kingdon Ward, Wilson, and the French botanist-priests Jean Pierre Armand David and Jean Marie Delavay. With his command of Chinese, and the local dialects which he could soon speak, he recruited assistants and established relationships with local potentates like the King of Muli. Support from various American sources – the Arnold Arboretum and the National Geographic Society in particular – kept him going year by year.

And he needed the money. Rock was never one to suffer in the field. When he went on an expedition, he normally moved in some state, with a train of horses and carriers. His equipment included a folding bathtub from Abercrombie & Fitch, and he made a practice of dressing for dinner, which was prepared to his orders by a specially trained cook and consumed with silver cutlery from china laid on a linen-covered table. His rationale was 'face'. As he once remarked, 'You've got to make people believe you're someone of importance if you want to live in these wilds.' That may not have been overstating the case: Rock's diaries are full of stories of marauding warlord armies, brigands, renegade armed priests and general disorder. More than once his plans were disrupted by fighting, political and otherwise, which deeply offended his Austrian sense of civil propriety.

In 1927, a funding crisis arose with the death of Charles Sargent, Rock's main backer at the Arnold Arboretum. In the nick of time, he managed to secure a commission from the Geographic Society to explore unmapped mountains west of Likiang. One expedition almost suffered disaster when an unseasonable hailstorm destroyed barley crops and the natives blamed it on the Rock party; they had been circling the sacred mountains in an anti-clockwise direction, which every good Tibetan knows is blasphemous. But it was during this trip that Rock got his first glimpse of an enormous mountain called Minya Konka. Could it be the highest mountain in the world?

In March 1929, confident that this time he had made a seriously important discovery, Rock set off on an expedition with Geographic Society backing to find out. Minya Konka – which he later diplomatically renamed Mount Grosvenor in honor of the president of the Society – had been seen and reported before from a distance, but never measured. Climbing it was out of the question, so Rock took bearings from surrounding high points with a variety of instruments before reaching his triumphant conclusion. 'Minya Konka Highest Peak On Globe 30,250 Feet Rock', said the cable to the Society. As it turned out, it wasn't. Rock's enthusiasm had run away with him again. Mount Grosvenor, while a considerable protuberance, was roughly a mile shorter than Rock's calculation, and no rival to Everest.

Rock might be excused not noticing the Wall Street crash, but it had a direct effect on his income. Moreover, the editors of the *National Geographic* were getting restive. 'Imagination he has none. Or form,' wrote one bedevilled rewrite man. 'Apparently he has never learned to write with a view to holding reader interest.' Possibly because of this, his contributions (after one leaden effort entitled 'Konka Risumgongba: Holy Mountain of the Outlaws') ceased. Plant collecting and exploring (on a reduced stipend) continued, but more and more Rock focused on his main interest, the ethnology of the Na-khi people living in the region around Likiang.

Floods, roaming hordes of leaderless soldiers, inflation, toothaches – all these made Rock's life unpleasant. He even fell back on speculating in currency, and of course lost money. The approach of war unsettled him completely. Three times he packed up his entire huge library and shipped it to Dalat in French Indochina, only to ship it back to Likiang again. His luck did not improve. Plates for one major work were destroyed by Japanese bombs at a printer in Shanghai, while all his notes and manuscripts – the fruit of twelve years of labour – went to the bottom when the ship carrying them to Europe was torpedoed. Yet apart from two years spent working for the United States Army Map Service in Calcutta, Rock stayed on in Likiang. He was still there in 1949, when the Communists chased him out for good, an unhappy man as usual. He retreated to Hawaii, and devoted his last years to reconstructing his lost papers, including a Na-khi dictionary.

It isn't easy to get the measure of Joseph Rock as a plant hunter. Significantly, he never published so much as a single paper on Chinese plants, though he worked with them for nearly half a century. Apart from the peony, gardeners know little of his introductions, yet on one trip alone he collected 6,000 chestnut seedlings in hope of finding a blight-resistant strain. Hundreds of plant varieties bear his name. And in Likiang his memory as a plantsman lives on. In his book *Travels in China*, Roy Lancaster tells of meeting a very old man there who remembered Rock. Because of ill-health (that bad stomach?) Rock had employed villagers to hunt plants for him. But he was the only one who could tell them what to look for.

Canon Ellacombe

GIVEN A FACILITY FOR WRITING SERMONS (and they didn't have to be either long or learned) life as a village rector in nineteenth century England must have been enviable. If you were a gardener, so much the better. No doubt you already occupied the nicest house for miles around, probably a comfortable old vicarage surrounded by two or three acres of land and a collection of ancient trees. Money was usually no problem – you could call on local help when you needed your lawn scythed or your shrubs pruned. In fact, wrote Henry Ellacombe, 'A country parson without some knowledge of plants is surely as incomplete as a country parsonage without a garden. . . . Such a man must be wretched . . . but I have not much pity for him.'

Canon Ellacombe had a right to feel superior. Amid a galaxy of clergyman-gardeners, he was outstanding, a plantsman whose reputation had, by the time of his death in 1916 at an age approaching 100, far outgrown the confines of his modest garden in a Gloucestershire village.

Part of Ellacombe's fame stemmed from his achievements as a gardener – he was an expert horticulturist responsible for collecting and growing many rarities and new varieties. But at least as much may be laid to his books, particularly the small classic called *In a Gloucestershire Garden*, first published in 1895. Packed with wise observations, comments on plants, aphorisms and attractive moralities, it combines a fresh and easy prose style with the stuff of nostalgia, serving to fix, as if in amber, the very essence of a parsonage garden a century ago.

Apart from his years at Oxford, and a short period as a curate in Derbyshire, Henry Ellacombe spent his entire life in Bitton, a tiny village between Bristol and Bath*. His father – a scholarly expert on

---

* Because of boundary-shifting, Bitton is no longer in Gloucestershire, but in Avon.

bell-ringing and by all accounts a considerable gardener – had been vicar there, and had started the garden which his son inherited. (An old document dated 1830 lists no less than 208 different roses.) 'I have in mind,' Ellacombe was to write, 'a garden of small extent', and the famous garden was exactly that: only 1½ acres, including the vegetable patch.

Universally known as the Canon – a title he received when he was made an honorary canon of Bristol Cathedral in 1881 – Ellacombe had what must be described as a deeply unexciting life. One searches in vain for a dramatic narrative. He married, his wife bore 10 children, he made a regular habit of composing a set of Latin verses while resting before dinner (which he would then recite to the family and guests), he went on jaunts to the Continent with one or another of his children, he fished and hunted and collected plants. Before taking over from his father in 1850, he even seems to have preferred genealogy to gardening, producing 'beautiful paintings of coats of arms'. In the words of one slightly despairing memoirist, 'Full of interest and beauty as was his life, it was not eventful in the ordinary sense of the term.'

While in this respect he was typical of many younger sons of the gentry who chose to enter the church, Ellacombe – as he makes plain from his book – found abundant excitement close to home, among his plants. He apparently had little or no interest in what he dismissed as the 'artistic' side of gardening, but rather treasured the individual plant – its beauty, its health, its exact preferences as to placement and soil. Beyond that, he wanted to understand it botanically, and find out all he could about its natural history and its associations with humans. If necessary (and it usually was necessary, because he had absolutely no room to spare) a single specimen of a given variety would do, though he was as a rule determined to find a sample of every different kind available. 'Each little flower meant so much to him,' wrote the great botanist W. J. Bean in his description of Bitton. 'It would be impossible to find another garden of its size so rich in species and varieties of hardy flowers and shrubs. . . . The collector spirit held him to the very end.'

So although it was 'wholly devoid of design', Bitton represented an amazing concentration of rarities. Bean estimated that over the fifty years before his death, Ellacombe grew nearly 3,000 different species or varieties there. In a five-year period in the 1870s alone, he received about 4,900 plants and 1,000 packets of seeds from various private individuals and botanical gardens from Kew to New York to Berlin and Gibraltar. Many found a home at Bitton, or at the very least had a good crack at growing in the limy earth and comfortable climate that prevailed there, sheltered between the Cotswolds and the Mendips.

In the days before specialist nurseries, such exchanges of plants were commonplace, and did much to knit together the gardening community. Ellacombe was a great believer in sharing his rarities, on the principle that 'no garden could flourish that was not constantly giving'. He was on close terms with successive directors of Kew through much of his life, for example, and was proud to have supplied examples of nearly two dozen rare plants for illustration in Kew's magisterial *Botanical Magazine*. Yet there was not much of the cool and objective scientist about him. He did not hesitate to express his likes and dislikes, the latter of which were famously numerous. Those plants he rejected out of hand were alone said to be sufficient to fill a border. ('A border?' one acquaintance commented. 'You'd be nearer the mark if you said an acre.') They included florist's tulips ('always coarse and flaring') and what he considered 'the ugliest object of all', a bed of double zinnias.

Similarly, the Canon's favourite plants show a wonderful inconsistency, ranging from sentimental attachment to admired oddity. In her contribution to a collective memoir, the distinguished gardener Ellen Willmott listed some of them. There was a black pansy brought from Italy by Ellacombe's father; *Statice cosirensis* (now *Limonium cosyrense*) grown from seeds brought to England by a sailor who had been in the Bitton choir as a boy; a fine *Viburnum tomentosum* var. *mariesii* (now *V. plicatum*); *Fremontodendron californicum* (which Ellacombe was the first to grow outdoors in England); a convolvulus said to have been raised from seeds found in the pocket of a drowned sailor; and a number of old roses, particularly *Rosa hemisphaerica*, the sulphur rose. Other visitors to Bitton in springtime noted his one concession to display – a grand spread of *Anemone blanda* in all forms, including doubles that he was the first to record. Many wildlings get a good word from the Canon, though not lesser celandines, which he regarded as 'a sad weed'. For someone so interested in unusual plants, he was at heart conservative, preferring old standard varieties, and often inveighing against unnecessary innovations.

In several ways, the Canon was ahead of his gardening time. Conifers were very fashionable in late Victorian England; he had 'no great love for them'. He believed in letting hardy plants fend for themselves: 'I dislike all tyings and nailings, all sticks, and everything that tends to cramp the free growth of the plants.' The modern practice of letting clematis clamber through and over shrubs and trees was old hat to him, and he argued for more climbers to be allowed to go where they would 'by their own unassisted powers' – including several types of climbing asparagus!

Friends spoke of Ellacombe's 'robust vitality'. This could sometimes take a startling form. He once went on a trout fishing and plant collecting trip to Ireland, commenting in a letter home: 'Went fishing by myself. It was not a good day, but I managed to get about five dozen.' 'Throw it away!' was his usual response to the offering of a plant he didn't like the look of. Nor was a plant necessarily safe in his own border. Suddenly annoyed by its appearance, he might pull it out bodily and discard it, only to replant it later. Much as he loved to have visitors, claiming that Bitton could supply some special beauty in every season, indeed every month, he could be sharp with anyone who he sensed was merely faking interest. When one lady simpered, 'Oh, Canon Ellacombe, what do you do to have all these beautiful flowers?' he answered forthrightly. 'Well, madam, I plant 'em.'

Still, from his writings and from the recollections of his many friends, it is plain that Ellacombe was a loveable and much-loved man, happy in his garden and his well-used library. His wisdom was of a kind that has an engaging – and lasting – charm. 'The garden,' he wrote, 'is a constant pleasure, and . . . the pleasure does not depend on unbroken success.' And again: 'The true gardener is never overmuch disquieted by bad seasons, whether they are seasons of frost or drought. . . . Bad seasons are a trial of his faith.' His three prerequisites for a gardener 'wishing to have and keep a good collection of plants' are patience, liberality and a catalogue.

Needless to say, the Canon possessed all three. He was over ninety when a visitor noted his experiments with supposedly lime-loving rhododendrons just arrived from Edinburgh, having had no luck with rhododendrons in sixty years. (He refused to use peat, though Ashmore, his frustrated gardener, is supposed to have smuggled in a load during the dead of night on one occasion.) His staying powers as an elderly man were legendary. Well into his eighties, he delightedly reported hearing from a French doctor in Paris that 'your heart is *splendide*; it does belong to a strong man of twenty'. Continental jaunts became, if anything, more adventurous.

At the advanced age of eighty-one, Canon Ellacombe undertook to cross a remote Alpine pass on an equally elderly horse. It is pleasant to hold in mind this picture of the hale old fellow, recorded by the much younger friend who accompanied him:

> We pushed on through deepish snow to the top of the next ridge, and on the other side we got into a tangle of torrents running through boulders and rhododendron scrub, and to add to our difficulties it thundered and rained for all it was worth. The Canon was quite placid, sitting on his horse as if he were part of it (it was often as not on its head or its knees!), a huge cotton umbrella over his head, and continually shouting, 'Baker! Baker! What's that flower?'

Reginald Farrer's Last Journey

I N ONE OF HIS FINAL LETTERS, to his cousin and boyhood friend
Osbert Sitwell, Reginald Farrer described his situation:

> Right away over on the far side of the uttermost edge of nowhere, I sit in
> a little bamboo shanty, open at every pore to all the winds that blow,
> surrounded, far overhead, by inky black peaks like flames in a tempest,
> frozen suddenly. . . . So now I'm happy as the day is long, working hard
> among the plants, and camping on high passes, full of snow and midges.

The year was 1920, the place Upper Burma, in the midst of virtually
unexplored mountains on the Chinese frontier. Reginald Farrer was
forty, author of half a dozen novels – mostly unreadable – and twice as
many irresistibly prolix, colourful, inspiring, opinionated and
influential books on plants, plant-hunting and rock gardens. In a few
weeks he would be dead.

The annals of plant collecting are full of odd characters, but it would
difficult to find one who combined quite as many oddities as Reginald
Farrer. He was born the scion of a wealthy Yorkshire family and grew
to be a handsome (if slightly bulky) man, blighted by a hare lip that
neither painful surgery nor a large moustache could wholly mask. His
voice was high-pitched. Sitwell found it 'as startling as the discordant
cry of a jay or woodpecker'. But his mind moved with huge agility and
he was never, ever, at a loss for words.

From childhood Farrer was a loner. He loved wandering over the
high limestone fells near his home, finding and puzzling over alpine
plants. When he was only fourteen the Journal of Botany noted his
discovery of a rare Arenaria, and a few years later he found an
unrecorded hybrid saxifrage, the first of many plants to bear his name.
He started his own rock garden, and at Oxford helped a fellow alpine
enthusiast to construct a sizeable one at St John's College, all the time

gaining increasingly detailed knowledge of the horticultural demands of plants from high places. It apparently never occurred to him, however, to engage in any formal botanical study.

More or less simultaneously, Farrer decided to become a traveller and a writer. His first long journey, immediately upon leaving Oxford, took him to China and Japan and yielded a book called *The Garden of Asia: Impressions from Japan* (1904). Like his later books, it rejoiced in sharp descriptive phrases that often drifted into pure purple, and displayed a truly exceptional ability to talk about individual plants in memorable terms. Not all of his readers appreciated this. One obituarist observed that 'he wrote vividly, often at the top of his voice, as it were . . . he always had something to say'. What is amazing is that so much of what he said remains highly original and engaging.

Tossing off a couple of novels in the interim, in 1907 Farrer published the first – and most reprinted – of his gardening books, *My Rock Garden*. It is a blend of how-to and sharply expressed opinion, largely in support of his own plantsman's approach, in which the rock structure should come second to the cultural demands of the alpines. This position was to be elaborated later in his magnum opus, the vast two-volume compendium of rock plant description and celebration, *The English Rock Garden* (1919). Never one for tact, Farrer managed to anger a number of contemporaries with skillful attacks on their rock gardens ('bald and chaotic barrenness'), while reviewers occasionally balked. ('We have seldom met with a work wherein the author's self-satisfaction was so conspicuous.')

Around 1907, influenced by his oriental travels (or possibly his instinctive wish to be different), he became a Buddhist and made a trip to Ceylon to visit some of the shrines. Subsequent journeys, often to the Alps and frequently in the company of fellow gardener Edward Augustus Bowles, were for the more worldly purpose of collecting plants. Farrer was a great believer in plant collecting, convinced that even the rarer species would never suffer extinction. 'If all the collectors in all the world with all their sacks, combined to toil at the task for months and years, I do not believe they could strip even one range of the Alps of their *Eritrichium*,' he wrote in *Among the Hills*, a delightful account of clamberings in the Swiss, French and Italian Alps. (Such an attitude would doubtless be frowned upon today, but the fact is that the gem-like blue *Eritrichium nanum* is a good deal easier to collect than to propagate.)

Much as Farrer enjoyed his Alpine jaunts, the idea of actually finding new and unknown species fascinated him. Not just any species, of course, but plants that would be both hardy in the British climate and worthwhile for gardeners to grow. (Farrer disdained 'weeds', even weeds that nobody had ever seen before.) Hard terrain held no terrors for him. 'He would walk,' a friend observed, 'with an odd little swagger, perfect grace, fearless poise, even in the worst places, and quite tirelessly.'

His first target, reached just before the outbreak of World War I, was the mountains of Northwest Kansu Province in China, where he went with the experienced plant hunter William Purdom. The expedition was a success, at least to the extent that Farrer and Purdom emerged alive in spite of the unsettled political conditions, brigands and warlike monks, and Farrer got a couple of books out of it (*On the Eaves of the World* and *The Rainbow Bridge*). But the war meant that relatively few of the plants they introduced survived into cultivation. Among those that did were *Geranium farreri*, *Gentiana farreri*, and *Buddleja davidii* var. *nanhoensis*.

Returning to wartime England in 1915, Farrer worked in the Ministry of Information, wrote, and corrected *The English Rock Garden*. No sooner did hostilities end, however, than he was off again to the Far East. This time, choosing a search area was much more difficult. Plant hunters better known (and funded) than Farrer were already at work in the choicest spots – E. H. 'Chinese' Wilson in Hupei and Szechuan, George Forrest in Yunnan and Frank Kingdon Ward all over the place, from Tibet to Burma. Nor would any old place do. The locale had to be remote and rich in unfamiliar plants, and also – especially in South Asia – high enough to encourage the sort of hardiness needed to survive European winters. Plant hunting was, after all, a business. Commercial nurserymen, botanical gardens, and syndicates of rich amateurs put up the money and in return expected beautiful objects they could sell or grow.

The area left for Farrer and his companion, E. M. H. Cox, was the peculiarly inhospitable range of high mountains running north–south along the edge of Burma, just west of the long gorge of the Salween River. This was not totally virgin territory, but it was so dense with vegetation that a great deal remained to be found. As Cox put it later, in a book about the venture, 'The truth is that the whole country is overgrown: it is nothing more than a giant propagating bed.' Much of the landscape was either jungle or – above 10,000 feet – smothered in an endless blanket of scrub bamboo and rhododendron. Yet some of the rhododendrons were new, while higher up a wide variety of alpines grew amid the screes and pocket meadows.

During the first season, Cox kept Farrer company, working out of a government post in the village of Hpimaw. Living conditions were acceptable – the police bungalow where they stayed at least shed the incessant rain – but there were other drawbacks: bamboo ticks 'the size of young crabs', snakes (when Farrer stepped on a ball of newly-hatched snakelets, Cox notes, 'it was the only time I have seen him flustered'), blister flies, not to mention the boredom of waiting for the weather to clear so that they could explore the high passes. In collecting terms, the summer was a fair success – a large number of rhododendrons (though nothing to compare with Forrest's finds, and few that reached cultivation back home), gentians, primulas (including the fabled *P. agleniana*, subsequently lost), *Nomocharis pardanthina*, and possibly best of all, Cox's Chinese coffin tree, *Juniperus recurva* var. *coxii*.

That winter, after the seed harvest, Cox went back to England, and Farrer stayed on, determined to go still further north in spring. This time he travelled alone, accompanied only by his Gurkha majordomo Bhaju and some bearers, into an extremely difficult region near the point where Burma, India and China come together. Regular reports to the *Gardener's Chronicle* in London described his adventures in getting there, and the near-impossibility of working in one of the world's most sodden places. On the Shing Hong Pass, after a hard four-day walk: 'For now I have lived for ten days in an unvarying fog of soaking rain. . . . It was all deadness, lit by the pale glare of the drenching fog.' On the Chawchi Pass in July: 'I took my camp to 12,000 feet and affixed it, like a temple-haunting martlet's nest, to some rocks below the pass . . . for the whole of my three weeks up there it never ceased to pour with rain but once for an hour.' Yet the plant-hunter's dream kept him going: 'To these delights, too, are invariably added those of always feeling that there must be a sky-blue rhododendron or a pea-green primula somewhere just out of sight, in the unfathomable white gloom.'

So far as we know – none of his seeds and few of his herbarium specimens from that last season ever reached Britain – Farrer never found his sky-blue rhododendron. His reports to the *Chronicle* and the letters he wrote to friends speak of many other wonders – a 'citron-coloured' fritillary, 'a *Meconopsis* of the integrifolia persuasion,' *Rhododendron aperantum* ('It is simply one of the most radiantly lovely things you ever saw'), 'an unspotted *Nomocharis* with flowers of a tone unknown to me in all hardy *Liliaceae*, of a pure salmon flame-colour,' and dozens more, described with inexhaustible (perhaps one should say undampened) enthusisasm. As had happened before, some of them would doubtlessly have turned out to be already known; Farrer's lack of formal botanical training sometimes tripped him up. But no botanist ever loved plants better than he did, or discussed them with greater joy.

As autumn 1920 drew on, he ended his last dispatch to the *Chronicle* by noting that exploration was nearly over and 'nothing will be left to do but rest and gather strength again, against the final whirlwind of the harvest'. He was already making new plans – for a trip to Nepal and Tibet on the one hand, and on the other to get married (he asked his college friend Aubrey Herbert to help find him a wife). But the harvest never came. On 1 October, huddling for cover in his bamboo shanty surrounded by specimens that he was trying to dry before shipment, Farrer fell ill. Little more than two weeks later he died, in spite of his majordomo Bhaju's valiant but fruitless attempt to get help from the nearest fort, five or six days and a flooded river away. The official cause was diptheria, though Cox doubted it, considering the remoteness of the place and the fact that it was virtually uninhabited.

When it was all over, as he reported in a letter to Cox, Bhaju saw to it that Farrer was buried 'with as very careful as much as I can', and then supervised the packing of what he regarded as Farrer's most valuable effects – the tents, the remaining tinned goods and other supplies, his frying pan and his boots, 'all the furnitures of my master'.

Less important things had to be left behind: 'there were many kinds of flowers and seeds there . . . and we could not bring them off.'

A great many plants bear Reginald Farrer's name today; the botanical historian William Stearn listed no less than twenty-nine, ranging from *Allium cyathophorum* var. *farreri* to *Viburnum farreri*. Yet on the whole his talents as a plant-hunter could not compare with men like Forrest or Wilson, nor was he a great gardener in an age of great gardeners. What made him memorable – and still does – was his enthusiasm. If it occasionally led him into excess (he could describe a modest little *Omphalogramma*, for example, in terms to make an advertizing man blush*, it nevertheless brought into the world of horticulture a rare and lasting kind of excitement. We need that as much as we need a blue rhododendron.

* 'Nor does it lag in beauty . . . here the emarginate turned-back lobes are in sixes or sevens, narrow, more or less entire, broadening to the cleft at their end, and the colour is superb, being really less of a violet blue than of real sapphire, or very dark, cornflower one. . . . Like stars of blue velvet midnight . . .' etc. etc.

Geoff

THE FIRST TIME I MET the late Geoff Hamilton was at, of all places, a Royal Horticultural Society flower show. He looked a bit shy and bemused, not at all the smiling confident fellow I had come to know from *Gardeners' World* on television. I went up and introduced myself and explained that I'd like a chance to interview him for an American gardening magazine. After all, he was by far the most famous gardener in Britain, and most Americans – like me before I moved here – had never heard of him. He amiably suggested I pay him a visit at Barnsdale.

Given Hamilton's ubiquity in the gardening media – prime time Friday night television, up to five magazine pieces a month, half a dozen books (every one a bestseller) – his almost total obscurity outside the UK was curious. Other famous gardeners – from Rosemary Verey and Penelope Hobhouse to Christopher Lloyd, Stephen Lacey and Roy Strong – are known and admired in America, their books read and their lectures attended. But of Geoff – nothing.

It was partly in search of an answer to this riddle that I drove up to Rutland one dim November day a few years ago, and found Hamilton's house at the end of a muddy and totally unmarked lane. (The lack of a sign was deliberate, he explained, a matter of self-defence. If he were ever foolhardy enough to hold an 'Open Garden' day, 50,000 Geoff Hamilton fans might well show up.) Autumn was what passed for a quiet time in Hamilton's schedule. Broadcasts were over for the winter. He had nothing to do but prepare for *Gardeners' World* and the next special series, write another book, write one of his weekly pieces for *Radio Times* or the *Daily Express*, or a monthly one for *Country Living* or *Gardeners' World* magazine, supervise the gardeners (three or four working full-time), sleep, eat. . . . A tiger for work, Hamilton had already suffered one heart attack, and was supposedly slowing down.

We walked in his garden, and talked about gardening and gardening on television. There was no mistaking his enthusiasm for the subject; he had loved growing things since he was a boy, and through years of work as a gardening journalist before becoming a television star. Yet if a man's garden is an expression of his personality, as some would maintain, Hamilton's was a fairly unsettling mixture. The nearest thing to landscaping was a long grass alley flanked by perennial beds, with an urn at the far end. For the rest there was a whole array of small square gardens framed by fences and hedges and little copses of scrubby trees, the horticultural detritus of many television programmes – two 'cottage gardens', a potager, a partially-finished 'hermitage' garden and a parterre. These were kept for sentimental reasons, and the possibility that they might come in handy in a future series. Clearly, Barnsdale was a garden with its head on its shoulders, a garden that meant business.

And so did Hamilton. He spent a lot of time, he admitted, trying to get the right level of sophistication for his television programmes and books. 'You have to show authority, of course, but you also have to appear to be learning. There are too many different kinds of gardeners, and the only thing they have in common is *interest*. Getting the level right is a constant dilemma. In the end you have to make a programme for yourself.'

Anybody who watched Geoff on *Gardeners' World* on Friday nights knows that this meant plenty of basic (if ingenious) how-to items from building a compost bin to tips for potting up narcissi, along with a quantity of notably un-woolly commentary on horticultural practicalities. You wouldn't be likely to find Geoff wandering through Sissinghurst languidly discussing the *Rosa longicuspis* or comparing *Carya illinoinensis* with *C. myristiciformis*. On the contrary, he seemed far more at home on an allotment, possibly chatting with old George Flatt, the ancient Suffolk pensioner he found for the 'Cottage Garden' series. Hamilton's hypothetical viewer, whom he claimed to keep in mind whenever working up a new project, was 'a sixty-five- to seventy-year-old widow who knows a bit about horticulture and how to use a hammer, saw, and screwdriver.'

I suggested that this approach put him rather at odds with the *gratin* of British gardeners and gardening writers, what he himself called 'the

Rosemary Vereys of this world.'

'Those people are great artists,' he replied, 'no question about it. But they're daunting. What worries me about them is that they give you the feeling that you ought to be able to do what they do, and make you feel bad if you can't. I want to make gardening accessible. We need the peak as something to aspire to, but I want to broaden its base.' He was cheered by the fact that Royal Horticultural Society membership had 'rocketed' in recent years, but it was not difficult to sense an undertone of annoyance with the organization, long identified as an exclusive club for lady and gentleman gardeners. His own relationship with it had its ups and down. He treasured the memory of the time one of the 'toffs' complained that *Gardeners' World* had 'lost its way', because 'they were always talking about potatoes'. Perhaps better than most people, Hamilton knew that potatoes were exactly what his viewers wanted to talk about.

Ironically, given the chance a lot of American gardeners would have probably felt the same way. The familiar problem is that potatoes and allotments are rarely associated with Britain in the mind of Americans dosed on BBC costume dramas, tales of country house life, and other anachronisms. My fellow countrymen are instinctively drawn instead to what you might call the aristocracy of the spade, that hereditary peerage of experts and proprietors of old and famous gardens everybody can admire and envy. After all, Americans are terrible snobs.

It's a pity. Just as the vast majority of British gardeners embraced him with enthusiasm, Geoff Hamilton would probably have 'gone down a treat' (to use one of his favourite sayings) in Terre Haute or Ypsilanti, if some broadcaster had tried. Now we'll never know. In any event this American will miss him.

Henry Ward Beecher

SCANDAL ISN'T SOMETHING YOU CONNECT with gardens, except possibly the Garden of Eden, and in that case the gardener Himself wasn't to blame. Whatever the birds and bees get up to among the dahlias, devotees of horticulture are conventionally regarded as models of propriety. At least they are supposed to have other things on their minds.

The fact is, however, that the central figure in the most sensational bedroom scandal of nineteenth-century America was a gardener – not only a gardener, but the author of one of the most engaging and popular gardening books of its time. Of course Henry Ward Beecher possessed other distinctions too – he happens to have been the richest, most famous and most listened-to preacher in the country, in an era when a good preacher was the equivalent of a pop star today. But he was a gardener first and last, if not foremost.

According to what must be a prizewinner in the category of blindly adulatory biographies, written by members of his family just after his death in 1887, Beecher's affection for flowers manifested itself at an early age, when he and his brothers ate a sackful of his mother's tulip bulbs under the impression that they were onions. The scolding, he remembered, focused on what he had missed in not seeing the blossoms. Whether this episode is what convinced him to take up horticulture is unknown, but by the time he was in his teens he was busily cultivating a plot of his own. (He even had one at boarding school.) At the same time, of course, he was developing very considerable skills as an orator, and contemplating the ministry.

Preaching ran in the family. His father, Lyman Beecher, was a New England Calvinist clergyman best known for his tirades against intemperance and duelling. His outspoken sisters included Harriet, author of *Uncle Tom's Cabin*, and Catherine, a distinguished advocate of education for women. Two older brothers were already ministers. High-mindedness among the Beechers was taken for granted, along with vigour of expression. In his earliest pastorates, first in a small Indiana town and then in the growing city of Indianapolis, Beecher followed the family tradition, preaching hell-fire sermons, conducting revival meetings, and generally keeping the devil at bay.

He married, and children were on the way when, possibly because money was short, he agreed to take on a unlikely spare time job as editor of a monthly magazine called *Indiana Farmer and Gardener*. It was apparently a respite from too much preaching, but it also satisfied his love for horticulture and nature in general. 'This employment of waste hours,' he would later write, 'not only answered a purpose of soothing excited nerves, but brought us into such relations to the material world, that, we speak with entire moderation, when we say that all the estates of the richest duke in England could not have given us half the pleasure which we have derived from pastures, waysides, and unoccupied prairies.' Under his guidance, in a very short time the magazine became the most popular farm publication in the whole Midwest.

I have never read one of Henry Ward Beecher's sermons, nor am I likely to, but I found his book of pieces from the *Indiana Farmer*, later collected and published under the title *Plain and Pleasant Talk about Fruit, Flowers and Farming*, to be a delight. There is nothing churchy about it, no over-padded meditations on the ways of God to man, very few 'gems' of poetry and no sententiousness. (One entry even goes so far as to attack 'fine writing about rural affairs' as 'painted emptiness'.) Instead, Beecher is crisp and funny and down-to-earth on a huge variety of subjects ranging from whether or not fruit trees should be cultivated (probably not, because it encourages excessive growth) to 'horticultural curiosities' (rhododendrons, fuchsias, tulips and alpine strawberries) to how to cook potatoes. Granted a good part of it consists of instructions – some of them of dubious value and quite a lot clearly lifted from some other sources – the entertainment value is unfailing high. You can see why he made a good preacher.

For example, he is skilful at nailing contemporary horticultural foolishnesses. 'It is said,' he observes, 'that pear-trees that are unfruitful, may be made to bear, by digging under them, cutting the tap root, and burying a black cat there. We do not know as it makes any difference as to the sex of the cat, though we should, if trying it, rather prefer the male cat.' He is equally dismissive of the practice of slitting the bark of a 'bark-bound' fruit tree – 'we should as soon think of slitting the skin on a boy's leg, or a calf, or a colt' – although (mysteriously) he is very keen about 'scraping and scouring the trunk and large branches' in lieu of spring pruning.

In general, though, Beecher is eager to help, and in those days before pesticides, help was needed. 'The climate of the West [i.e. the Midwest] is entirely glorious for all manner of insects,' he points out. 'They can put the East to shame in the matter of aphids, cockroaches, cutworms, army and wire-worms, curculios, peach-worms, grubs, [etc. etc.]' In particular it was the curculio beetle that caused the most dire problems, wiping out plum crops and doing signal damage to a variety of other fruits. His suggestion was to hit the tree a smart blow with a mallet, having first spread a sheet underneath to catch the insects when they fell. 'This should be performed when it is cool, as then, only, the curculio is somewhat torpid.' (Other treatments in vogue, incidentally, included building 'a tight board fence' nine feet high around the tree, boring a hole in the trunk and filling it with sulphur, or hanging planks dipped in tar from the branches. Beecher's system, by contrast, worked.)

It is clear from many passages in *Plain and Pleasant Talk* that his experience of farming and gardening was direct and personal. When he remarks that 'a seedsman's list, a nurseryman's catalogue, are more fascinating to us than any story,' he really means it. He always managed to find time for growing things. His biography quotes 'one old parishioner' from Indianapolis days as saying that Beecher 'always always had the earliest vegetables in the market, and his garden was better than any other in the city'. He knew the names of all the flowers, and won prizes for his squashes, beets and salsify (which he knew as oyster-plant). One of his beets, the parishioner reported, weighed fourteen pounds!

But his reputation as a preacher was growing, and in 1846 he was invited back East to take charge of a new church in fashionable

Brooklyn Heights. He never again wrote about gardening. Now a public figure of increasing influence and importance, he spoke out on slavery, women's suffrage, and most other large issues, meanwhile publishing copiously and drawing packed crowds to the Plymouth Church. With a large house in Brooklyn and, ultimately, a 36-acre estate called Boscobel in Peekskill, just north of New York City, he was not only the best-known and most admired minister in America by far, but also the wealthiest. He even harboured dreams of being nominated for the Presidency.

Beecher's gospel, famously, was 'love without stint' – spiritual love, that is. A heavy-faced man with lank grey hair down to his shoulders, he nevertheless retained by all accounts the boyish charm of his youth, and was especially attractive to his many devoted female admirers.

In retrospect, Beecher might have done better to stick to his hoe. In the early 1870s, when he was at the height of his fame, rumours began to circulate about certain unchurchly relationships. The young wife of a long-time colleague and friend named Theodore Tilton confessed to her husband that she and Beecher had been intimate. For a while the matter was hushed up (along with other similar charges) and might have remained so except for the activities of an extraordinary character named Victoria Woodhull, whose magazine *Woodhull and Claflin's Weekly* broke the story. Libel writs flew. Woodhull, a pioneer feminist infuriated by what she regarded as male hypocrisy, forced Tilton to sue, declaring 'I will make it hotter on earth for Henry Ward Beecher than Hell is below.'

Up in Boscobel, Beecher stolidly went on competing with his neighbour George Dayton over whose corn and peas would be earliest, and did his best to keep his English gardener's potato patch from encroaching on the hollyhocks and pinks. In Brooklyn, he continued his pastoral duties, rallying his supporters in private. But every newspaper and magazine in the country was full of the scandal, overflowing with savage cartoons and insulting jokes. In the end, in the face of all the evidence, Tilton lost his case – the jury was hung and the judge declared a mistrial – yet Henry Ward Beecher's halo had been dented beyond repair.

He went on preaching, he came out in support of the theory of evolution, he built a fine new house at Boscobel, he directed the planting of huge beds of roses, dahlias, phlox, geraniums, pansies, lilies and chrysanthemums. It was almost as if he was trying, by throwing himself back into the world of farming and gardening, to recover some of the purity and hopefulness of his youth. In 1887, he died. By then, the rural simplicities of *Plain and Pleasant Talk* must have seemed a long way away.

The Corncob Lab

M OST GARDENERS HAVE HEARD of Linnaeus, and even the ones who haven't most likely make use (if reluctantly) of the binomial system of plant names he invented to make sense out of the terminological jumble of the eighteenth-century plant kingdom. The same can hardly be said, however, of the Philadelphia grandee whom Linnaeus himself called the greatest botanist of the age.

Whether or not Linnaeus's praise was really merited (he was sometimes given to over-enthusiasm) the fact remains that fame has escaped James Logan. This is a pity. He was quite a fellow – merchant in furs, politician, self-taught mathematician, astronomer and investigator of optics, book collector, and (for our purposes) gardener and botanical experimenter. As a sort of universal polymath, in fact, Logan rivalled his younger Philadelphia friend Benjamin Franklin.

James Logan was born in Ulster in 1674, the son of a schoolmaster, and fled with his family to Scotland during the troubles connected with the Glorious Revolution of 1688. Several abortive attempts to settle in a career ensued, possibly disrupted by his passion for self-education – he taught himself six languages among other things. In 1699, however, William Penn hired him as his secretary, and took him off to the New World. For the rest of his life Logan served Penn and his successors in many colonial offices, built up a highly successful business of his own dealing in furs, invested profitably in land, ships, ironworks and securities, and spent the rest of his time – when there was any – at his estate of Stenton on the northern edge of Philadelphia, studying, pottering in his garden, and speculating.

This not the place to examine the full range of Logan's speculations, even if that were possible. He theorized about why lightning was jagged, and why the moon looked so much bigger when it was setting. He worked on the problem of determining longitude, and may have been the first American to learn calculus. He analyzed the moon's orbital motion and improved upon his hero Isaac Newton's *Opticks*. What drew Linnaeus's admiration above all, however, was Logan's work with plants, in particular one ingenious, simple, profoundly influential experiment.

It is easy to forget that much we take as obvious was once – and not very long ago in many cases – an outright mystery. A perfect example is the process of reproduction in plants. These days, with 'the birds and the bees' no more than a clichéd starting point for juvenile sex education, it is startling to realize that it has been scarcely three centuries since the role of pollen in fertilization was proposed, and a good deal less than that since it was widely accepted. As for the bees, although Aristotle in ancient Greece had noted the way that they fed on only one type of flower at a time, it was not until 1750 that an observant Irishman named Arthur Dobbs reported to the Royal Society his finding, based on a great deal of bee-watching, that 'Providence has appointed the Bee to be very instrumental in promoting the Increase of Vegetables' by carrying 'the *Farina* [pollen] from Flower to Flower.'

At the time James Logan was contemplating the mystery of plant reproduction, however, birds and bees were not yet a central issue. Argument focused instead on more basic matters. The male role in reproduction was generally taken to be the important one (Newton alone maintained, as Logan put it, that 'the animal is in the ovum') and the discovery of pollen suggested that it was the 'male seed'. What was known was that some sort of sexual fusion had to take place in most plants before fertile seed resulted. What was the mechanism for this? The stamens appeared to produce pollen, but what *is* pollen? Does it have to get to another plant, and if so how? And assuming that the pollen reaches the recipient plant, how does it get to the ovary?

One of the first to guess at the function of pollen had been the English botanist Nathaniel Grew, who harboured the delightful opinion that the stamens provided food for 'a vast number of little Animals . . . each Flower becoming their Lodging and their Dining-room, both in one'. A German professor named Camerarius went further, pinching out the anthers from male flowers of several species, among them mulberries and spinach, to demonstrate that in the absence of pollen the female plants wouldn't set seed. Richard Bradley, followed by the great gardener Philip Miller of the Chelsea Physic Garden (who suggested that insects might play a part in delivering pollen), did the same experiment with tulips. But acceptance was not universal: Joseph Pitton de Tournefort, the leading French botanist, maintained that pollen was nothing more than excess sap produced by the plant, excreted as unwanted by the stamens. He didn't believe fertilization was necessary anyway.

Despite conservatives like Tournefort, by the 1720s most scientific opinion favoured the idea that plants had to be pollinated, even those that seemed to have male and female parts in a single blossom. Establishing this with precision and numerical exactitude appeared an impossible challenge. But James Logan, fascinated by the new notion that plants might have 'male as well as female seed', found himself in 1727 in a position to do just that. After all, he had 'Mayze or *Indian Corn*' in his thoroughly American garden, and realized that this plant was uniquely suited to an experiment.

So when the ground could be worked in the spring, Logan planted four hills of corn, one in each corner of his 40- by 80-foot garden, and waited until the stalks were fully grown and 'pushing out Tassels above, and Ears below.' Then:

> . . . from one of those Hills, I cut off the whole Tassels, on others I carefully open'd the Ends of the Ears, and from some of them I cut or pinch'd off all the silken Filaments; from others I took about half, from others one fourth and three fourths,&c. with some Variety, noting the heads, and the Quantity taken from each: Other Heads I again tied up at their Ends, just before the silk was putting out, with fine muslin, but the Fuzziest or most Nappy I could find, to prevent the passage of the Farina; but that would obstruct neither Sun, Air or Rain. I fastened it so very loosely, as not to give the least Check to Vegetation.

The result was precisely what he had hoped. Checking his crop at the beginning of October, he found the muslin-wrapped ears empty of mature kernels, and the ears with parts of silk removed lacking in such kernels in exact proportion to the amount of missing silk. In the group where the tassels had been removed, the ears were small and light and filled with imperfect kernels, except for one ear facing in the direction of the prevailing wind that had apparently received pollen blown in from the other end of the garden.

Logan had proved several facts. First, pollination was necessary, and in the case of corn the pollen had to come from another plant. (Of course Logan still thought of pollen as the 'male seed', needing only to be 'planted' in the female to grow.) Second, the dust-like 'farina' could be carried from one plant to another by wind. Third, the filaments of cornsilk functioned as transmission pipes carrying the pollen to each kernel. It would be a hundred years before anyone was actually able to trace the passage of the microscopic pollen grain all the way from the receptor (the stigma) to the ovule, but Logan (who claimed to have seen a grain halfway down) established the process in principle.

Having repeated the experiment the next year, and rightly proud of the results he had achieved, he wrote a letter describing his findings to his fellow Quaker Peter Collinson in London for presentation to the Royal Society. It apparently did not meet with cheers of acclamation; according to one observer, while extracts from Logan's letter were being read two thirds of the members present were occupied in 'dissecting a German cabbage and looking for the small fibres in the root of an Indian turnip'. But it went down better with the international scientific community. Linnaeus quickly wrote a letter of praise and recommended that Logan's report be published. Before long it was – in Latin in Leiden in 1739, in English a few years later – and learned dissertations from Tübingen to St Petersburg were citing it.

Ironically in view of the scientific value of his experiments, it is now apparent from his letters that Logan was actually attempting to investigate something else, a fairly weird theory involving the riddle of creation itself. From an English theologian named William Wollaston, he had picked up the notion that 'the first Seeds, the true Essences of all beings' somehow exist, invisible but 'perfectly formed in the air & other parts of our Globe', ready to be taken up by the male element (in this case pollen) and carried along to take physical shape within the female.

Tinkering with his cornstalks didn't really prove this theory one way or the other, although it made clear to him that pollen was indeed indispensable to the generative process. In Logan's view, however, it remained plausible that *en route* to the female the pollen had collected 'out of the Air this little Seed or Plant, pre-existent and completely formed'. After all, stranger things were known to happen. And in any event, the fact that 'so wonderful a Structure should be the Effect of so simple a Process . . . exceeds the utmost Limits of human Apprehension'.

Logan's work was gradually left behind by more professional botanists, although it continued to be cited well into the nineteenth-century. The 'utmost limits of human Apprehension' proved to be infinitely more generous than he, husking corncobs in a Pennsylvania autumn, could have imagined. But he deserves to be remembered, if only for his irrepressible curiosity about the whole natural world. It was still with him at an age when most men would have happily retired to a chimney corner. 'The old man and Tom Godfrey are very busy in inspecting into a comet that has appeared for three weeks past,' wrote a Philadelphia acquaintance when Logan was approaching seventy. 'The public expect their opinion of it in print.'

John Evelyn's Elusive Elysium

O NE GLOOMY AUTUMN SUNDAY in the year 1665, the great diarist Samuel Pepys hired a boatman to take him a few miles down the Thames from London to Deptford, where he paid a visit to his friend 'Mr Evelings', a man better known to posterity as John Evelyn. Evelyn lived in a mansion called Sayes Court, a comfortable estate surrounded by spacious grounds; he was wealthy (the family money came from gunpowder) and enjoyed a reputation as something of a connoisseur. On this day he was apparently in a show-off mood. He displayed some paintings to Pepys; he explained – to the diarist's admiration – the new process of making a mezzotint; he read part of a play or two he had written, and some poems (they were, noted Pepys, 'not transcendent'); then, hauling out what must have been a very large stack of manuscript, Evelyn 'read to me very much also of his discourse he hath been many years and now is about, about Guardenage; which will be a most noble and pleasant piece.'

Above all else, above his interest in architecture, sculpture, engraving techniques, literature, science, theology, clean air (he wrote a pamphlet on London smog) and a dozen other subjects, John Evelyn was a gardener, possibly the most notable gardener of his time. (Pepys could take gardening or leave it.) Yet the project Evelyn was, as Pepys put it, 'about', a vast compendium of horticultural information, description and philosophy entitled *Elysium Britannicum*, would not see the light of day for nearly 300 years. Until very recently, it was probably the greatest garden book never published.

Gardening apparently fascinated Evelyn from the start. We find him as a young man in 1643, in the midst of the Civil War, successfully staying clear of battle by quietly redesigning the gardens at the family estate of Wotton in deepest Surrey. The diaries he kept during his travels on the Continent, which spanned years and extended from

Holland to Naples, are crammed with descriptions of the gardens and estates he made a point of visiting. Water features particularly delighted him, especially fountains and cascades and jokey devices such as hidden sprays to douse unwary guests. But he also gained great familiarity with the principles of Renaissance garden design, the groves and parterres and formal hedging still to be seen today at Versailles and other great French and Italian gardens. By the time he had married and purchased Sayes Court, he was ready to put what he had seen, learned, and thought about into practice for himself.

His first step was to acquire more land. This was, after all, the heyday of the great French landscape designer André Le Nôtre, whose influence was pre-eminent, and whose plans needed vast tracts in which to lay out perspectives and allées. (Evelyn himself – who had no interest in speaking to 'cabbage-planters' – once intimidatingly commented that 'something very princely, may be contrived in thirty akers.') He bought an adjoining 100-acre field and began making a garden.

Unusually, something is known of what Evelyn initially created at Sayes Court, because a plan of it dated 1653 survives among his papers. Trees were by far the most prominent element – he planted thousands, including large blocks of broad-leaf and an 'ortchard' of fruit trees. A 'grove' or 'wilderness' divided by avenues radiating from a central monument embodied one of his favorite notions – that by using nothing but evergreen trees and shrubs you could make a garden 'perpetually florid' even in the English climate, as in Italy 'where the Seasons are more benigne'. He also laid out a large oval parterre in the French style, with *broderie* in box and various herbs, made a 'mount' (an artificial hill), and planted a 'coronary' or flower garden along with a variety of hedges. He would later claim to have been the first to recommend the use of yew for topiary.

It seems likely that Evelyn was not really a hands-on gardener, nor, given his wealth, did he need to be. In his summary of the three things necessary for the making of garden – 'First, a good purse; Secondly, a judicious Eye; and thirdly, a skillfull hand' – he accounted himself possessed mainly of the first two. But he was keenly aware of the importance of practical knowledge, and from the start saw it as his duty to make such knowledge available where he could.

A first hesitant step along this route was the publication of a handbook by Nicolas de Bonnefons called *The French Gardiner*, which Evelyn translated with revisions and additions in 1658.

He must have already had in mind *Elysium Britannicum*, his 'Grand Hortulan design'. The dedication to *The French Gardiner* mentions it. Certainly the subject of his next book, one which made him famous, could fit right into the larger project. *Sylva; or A Discourse of Forest Trees and the Propagation of Timber in his Majestie's Dominions* (1664) was commissioned by the new Royal Society, of which Evelyn was a leading member. An eloquent and powerful argument for planting more trees, desperately needed for ship-building timber as well as for their beauty and healthfulness, *Sylva* also comprised a groundbreaking account of the characteristics and cultural needs of different species. The book became hugely popular, was reprinted many times, and is even credited with a role in Britain's naval victories a century later, since without Evelyn's beloved oaks Admiral Nelson would have had no ships.

Word about his great work of 'Guardenage' spread among Evelyn's friends. As early as 1659 he was being urged to finish it. But it apparently grew uncontrollably, with finished chapters giving rise to addenda on extra sheets of paper, then additions to the addenda on still more slips and scraps. In 1664, the same year as *Sylva*, he published a useful little handbook, *Kalendarium Hortense* ('Gardener's Almanack'), setting out the tasks to be performed in the garden throughout the year, the forerunner of dozens of similiar guides. That would presumably find a place in the *Elysium*. There was also *Acetaria: A Discourse of Sallets*, finally published separately in 1690, which deals with salad greens and dressings; and two appendices added to Sylva – a 'philosophical essay on earth' and a treatise on apple trees and cider.

Originally, Evelyn appeared to know what he was aiming at in *Elysium*. It was meant to consist of three books totalling forty-three chapters. The first book was to be on the soil and the seasons; the second on garden design and features; the third on preservation, distilling and descriptions of famous gardens. As time went on, however, the focus blurred, and sprouts of new subject matter shot off the main stems at every turn. In 1679, he wrote to a friend:

> When again I consider into what an ocean I am plunged, how much I have written and collected for above these twenty years on this fruitful and inexhaustible subject (I mean horticulture), not yet fully digested to my mind, and what insuperable pains it will require to insert the (daily increasing) particulars into what I have already to some measure prepared. and which must of necessity be done by my own hand, I am almost out of hope that I shall ever have the strength and leisure to bring it to maturity.

In 1690, he despairingly noted that his manuscript now added up 'to so enormous a Heap, as to fill some Thousand Pages'. Big subject, gardening.

Evelyn lived to be eighty-five, and virtually to the end of his life he was tinkering with *Elysium*. His years had not been altogether happy ones – of his nine children, only two survived to adulthood, and his various public services as a royal functionary had brought him little satisfaction. His garden, by contrast, seems to have been an unfailing joy, except for one terrible incident: in 1678, he was prevailed upon by James II to rent Sayes Court to the young Tsar Peter – later Peter the Great – who had come to England to learn the art of shipbuilding. Evelyn's bailiff reported that 'There is a housefull of people, and right nasty', which seems to be an understatement. The Russians smashed up the house and 'damnified' the garden, worst of all trundling each other in wheelbarrows straight through Evelyn's precious eight-foot holly hedge. It was enough to make any gardener give up and go back to the library.

After Evelyn's death, his papers – including the still-unpublished *Elysium* – passed through various more or less uninterested family hands. Some, no doubt, went to line pudding bowls and make dress patterns, the usual fate for unwanted foolscap; some were auctioned or stolen; the rest, an unwieldy and disorganized mass, finally ended up at Christ Church College in Oxford, to be sold on to the British Library in 1995. Two bound volumes contained roughly a third of

Evelyn's masterwork, much of it in a far from final form. Conceivably, it is all that he ever finished; opinions about this differ.

To read what survives of *Elysium*, which is now possible thanks to a transcription heroically completed by the American scholar John Ingram*, is an experience at once fascinating, enlightening and sad. Fascinating because of the scale and mad comprehensiveness of the contents, which range from discussion of the Garden of Eden to instructions (illustrated with a drawing) for making a 'wind chest' to animate mechanical birds. Enlightening because of what it tells us about gardening practices three centuries ago, including lists of recommended plants (some of which can no longer be found), design hints, propagation and cultivation techniques, and much more. Sad, finally, because its unmanageable scope so plainly defeated its author, in spite of his decades of devoted labour. In the end, poor John Evelyn's work was anything but an *Elysium*.

---

* *Elysium Britannicum, or The Royal Gardens by John Evelyn*, edited by John E. Ingram. University of Pennsylvania Press (Philadelphia 2001).

Père Delavay

I HAD INTENDED TO WRITE A PIECE about the great Scottish plant-collector George Forrest, who spent nearly thirty years slogging through the bamboo jungles and across the screes of south-western China, Burma, and the edges of Tibet, braving hostile locals and breathtaking altitudes. Probably no single collector ever introduced so many new and spectacular plants: primulas, gentians, magnolias, and dozens more – above all, rhododendrons.

I still mean to write about Forrest one day. But something odd happened as I was looking into his exploits. I kept running into the name of another man, who almost invariably appeared to have found a given plant long before George Forrest came on the scene. While Forrest could indeed claim credit for making sure that viable seeds or corms or cuttings of new species reached Kew or Edinburgh or one of his wealthy plant-loving sponsors back home – an achievement heroic enough – time and again credit for the actual discovery went to an obscure French priest named Jean-Marie Delavay, who generally beat Forrest to the post by twenty or thirty years.

It's not easy to find out much about Delavay. No biography exists, as far as I know. He never published anything under his own name, and even French encyclopedias either ignore him or provide meagre information. Histories of Catholic missions in nineteenth-century China explain why Delavay happened to be where he was, but are of little help in explaining his extraordinary achievements as a plant-hunter.

The facts of his life are these. He was born in the town of Abondance in the French Alps in 1834, and ordained in 1860. In 1866, after serving as a parish priest in several small French villages, he decided to devote himself to mission work in China. The time was ripe for such a move; the joint British-French expedition to Peking in 1860 had not only defeated the Chinese armies and laid waste to the Summer Palace, but had forced the Chinese government to open many parts of the hitherto closed country to foreign traders and missionaries. Hopes of conversions were running high, especially among Catholics. Whole regiments of French and Italian priests headed east under the auspices of several missionary organizations. Delavay chose to enter the Missions Étrangeres de Paris.

For nearly fifteen years, he served in South China, in Guangdong and Guangxi provinces. There is no record of his success in making converts, but according to one source he occupied himself notably with saving Annamese women who had fallen victim to pirates and had been sold into slavery. Nor do we hear about any botanizing, though he doubtless did a certain amount of collecting, observing, and studying native species. (H. F. Hance, an Englishman living in China and interested in plants, apparently asked Delavay to collect for him.) In 1881, however, while on leave in France, he was introduced by another naturalist priest to Adrien Franchet, a botanist attached to the Musée d'Histoire Naturelle in Paris. Franchet, who specialized in Japanese and Chinese plants, wanted specimens, and Delavay agreed to send whatever he could find. (In view of the subsequent fate of many of his discoveries, it was an unfortunate decision.) He then set off for his new post in China, which unexpectedly turned out to be located in one of the richest, most interesting and, at the time, least known sources of temperate garden plants in the world.

The province of Yunnan was – and to some extent still is – a kind of frontier region. Remote and difficult to reach in the days before air travel, it is ridged with mountains that become higher the closer you get to the borders of Burma and Tibet. Except in a few large valleys, it is sparsely settled, and mostly with non-Chinese tribal people. Delavay's mission station was in such a valley, a few miles north and east of a lake called the Er Hai and a major town, Dali. Mountains stand all around, and it was these mountains that would yield their plant riches to him.

Much of what we know about Delavay's experiences during the thirteen years he spent at Dapingzi (meaning 'big flat' – in that country anything level is worth naming) must be guessed from the notations on the handwritten tags attached to the thousands of plant specimens he sent back to Paris. Most of them mention a location, although the combination of French-style pronunciation of Chinese and an eccentric transliteration system make many of the names difficult to identify. What is nevertheless clear is that Delavay roamed widely over the entire region in search of plants, scaling precipices and cutting through near-impenetrable forests. According to Emile Bretschneider, the Russian doctor who in 1898 published a now-dated but indispensable history of European plant discoveries in China, Delavay's wanderings covered no less than 2,000 square miles, much of it extremely rough country, extending from Dali north to Lijiang.

One particularly productive area seems to have been Cangshan, the mountain chain that rises to an altitude of nearly 14,000 feet west of the Er Hai. In *Travels in China, a Plantsman's Paradise*, Roy Lancaster describes a trip he made to the mountain in 1981, which gives some sense of what it must have been like for Delavay a hundred years earlier. Although most of the forest cover on the western slope has been destroyed, logged off without much thought for erosion, Lancaster and his companions found dozens of choice plants first reported by Delavay, from *Paeonia lutea* to *Osmanthus delavayi*. The terrain was no easier – tracks rather than roads, sheer-walled gorges, the best plants often growing in the least accessible places.

For his part, Delavay made light of difficulties. In a letter to Bretschneider, he claims to have hardly touched upon the riches of the region, and commends it to later explorers; you can get almost to the top of most of the mountains on horseback, he writes, the climate is very healthy, and food supplies are abundant, 'although the population, being unused to strangers, may not show themselves to be very hospitable'. (If George Forrest ever saw these words, he must have felt a moment of chagrin. His own journeys took him further west and north into the far more difficult country sliced by the Mekong and Salween gorges, and he almost lost his life to some especially inhospitable members of the population. They did in fact torture and kill several of Delavay's fellow missionaries.)

In all, Père Delavay sent Franchet some 200,000 specimens collected on the Cangshan and elsewhere, representing more than 4,000 different species. He prepared, dried, and labelled each one himself, with such skill and patience that one commentator has called him 'a supreme artist' in the painstaking procedure. It has been estimated that at least 1,500 of these represented entirely new and unknown species, and sometimes even new genera. The roll call of memorable discoveries is too long to give here, but it includes such treasures as *Incarvillea delavayi* (the finding of which, according to the acerbic Reginald Farrer, 'is almost enough to reconcile oneself to the existence of missionaries'); *Clematis chrysocoma*; *Thalictrum delavayi*; the famous blue poppy *Meconopsis betonicifolia*; *Magnolia delavayi*; *Prunus serrula*; *Deutzia discolor*; *Primula vialii*; dozens of gentians, corydalises and senecios; and an incredible range of rhododendrons, most of which are still in cultivation. Among the latter, *R. racemosum*, *R. haematodes*, and *R. campylogynum* later proved to be of particular value to breeders.

In a few cases – the *Incarvillea* and the *Deutzia*, for example – Delavay also managed to get ripe seeds to Paris. There, plants were successfully raised and eventually distributed to European gardeners but not without drama. Maurice de Vilmorin, the plant breeder and nurseryman, undertook to introduce *Osmanthus delavayi*, but of all the seeds he received only one germinated. It had to be propagated by grafting onto stocks of privet and *Phillyrea latifolia*, and it was years before Vilmorin had enough to sell. Tragically, most of the seeds Delavay sent were simply wasted through carelessness.

While it is true that he was first on the scene in Yunnan and thus in a position to steal a march on later collectors, it is still remarkable that he was able to achieve what he did in the space of only thirteen years. As a missionary, he also had pastoral duties, and these were apparently rigorous. In 1888, while fighting a local outbreak of bubonic plague, he was himself stricken, and never fully recovered. On the way back to France on leave in 1892, what must have been a stroke partially paralyzed him, but he insisted on returning to China and continuing to search for plants. In 1895, in Yunnan, he died.

Delavay's collections remained at the Musée d'Histoire Naturelle in Paris, where Franchet attempted, with mixed success, to describe and publish them. The botanist was frankly swamped. Other French missionaries had been sending him an increasing volume of specimens from various parts of China and he was having an impossible time trying to keep up. A lengthy article of 1885 summarizing Delavay's initial shipment was followed by two abortive book projects; *Plantae Delavayanae* (1890), the second of these, managed to get to the saxifrages before coming to a halt. In 1898 Bretschneider observed that although Franchet was continuing to describe 'Delavay's novelties' from time to time in French botanical journals, 'he seems still very far from mastering this vast collection.' Nor did Franchet ever master it: in 1900, he too died. Some specimens have never been catalogued.

Yet this was not the disaster it might have been. Professional collectors like Forrest and Frank Kingdon Ward were already moving into the field, proving – as Delavay had suggested – that there was much more to be found in Yunnan and south-western China. They faced, moreover, a new challenge, one that Père Delavay, for all his energy and bravery, was seldom able to meet: not merely to discover 'novelties', but actually to introduce them, in living form, to the gardens of the West.

HUSBANDRY

Machines

I got a new machine the other day – well, a third of a machine; the other two thirds belong to my farmer neighbour Jimmy McConnel, who to be honest has more need of it than I do. It's a kind of super mower, built on the general principle of a standard rotary mower, but far heavier, with a 26-inch blade made out of quarter-inch-thick steel, two fat cleated wheels, four speeds forwards and one in reverse, and 14 horsepower. It is called an all-terrain mower, and so far that seems accurate – I have not found any terrain yet that it can't mow, including a cut-over woodland area studded with stumps and blackberry/bracken thickets the size of houses. McConnel intends to use the machine for mowing between rows of Christmas trees; I wanted it for clearing the wood and for the once- or twice-a-year mowing of my putative wildflower meadow (see p. 32). Basically, though, I just wanted it.

It is hardly too much to say that I love machines. This goes against the grain of the British gardening ethos, which seems horrified by any machine much more substantial than a hand-propelled reel mower, but I don't care. I also know that my attitude is frightfully non-green, responsible for a variety of loud noises, exhaust fumes, and (depending on the machine involved) dangerous flying bits of gravel, twigs, molehills, hedge trimmings and other debris. I don't really care about that, either. The way I look at it, it's machines that make the garden possible. We only have weekends, and no gardener on call. (Okay, so there's a boy who comes to mow the lawn.) Where would we be without the hedge clipper? The oversized string trimmer? The four mowers? The chain saw? The rotovator? Why, without my machines . . .

Yet even as I write this, I know that I'm lying. I possess all these machines because machines fascinate, amuse and please me. They always have, ever since at the very end of World War II it became possible to buy a model aeroplane engine. The one I got was called, I think, a May, and in all the time I had it, I succeeded in making it run only once. This was not for want of trying. I still have scars on my knuckles from fruitlessly flipping a wooden prop mounted on the drive shaft, while it backfired. Later engines were better, and did much to inure me (though perhaps not my mother or the neighbours) to the sound of a muffler-less motor revving in the garage on a peaceful Sunday morning. It was good training in many ways – the noise, the smoke, the frustrations of poor ignition, stale fuel, and simple crankiness – for more recent experiences with bigger, and theoretically more practical, machines.

These days, my biggest machine of all is a rotovator. It must weigh at least 300 pounds, and has an 8 horsepower engine that has never failed me. (I must note in passing that I wouldn't have a beast like this if it weren't for the fact that my brother-in-law used to run a company that made them, and we did a deal.) The one problem with the rotovator lies not in the machine but in the nature of the soil and the climate in our corner of the Welsh Marches, i.e. sticky red clay, and lots of rain. The only time it works with perfect efficiency in the vegetable garden is in August, which is the only time of the year when the ground has dried out enough to till. And oddly enough there is very little reason to till a garden that is already full of green beans and courgettes. Try to till in April, in readiness for planting, and you have to spend at least half the time prying solid masses of clay off the tines. As for the tilth it produces, this consists mainly of fist-sized chunks that proceed to harden into terracotta.

Despite its dubious utility, however, I'm very fond of my rotovator. I've offered to let friends in the neighbourhood use it, but I notice a reluctance from them to do so. This probably has nothing to do with the clay issue; some people here have perfectly normal soil, having created it over the course of a few hundred years with applications of sheep manure. I'm tempted to think that they are put off by the rotovator's size, and the fact that it is, of course, a *machine*. You dig a garden with a spade, not a machine. Still, for my part I find that there's something comforting about seeing it sitting there in the corner of the garage, all ready to dig in whenever it's wanted.

I started out with a gas-powered hedge-clipper, a little one with a 14-inch sword. My reasoning when I bought it was that since I've got a lot of hedges, some of them quite a long way from the house, an electric model wasn't practicable, and a small machine would be easier to lift over the parts that have grown difficult to reach. My reasoning was faulty. The short sword frequently jammed and made cutting the high stuff worse than awkward – you had to burrow into one side of the hedge (seriously uncomfortable in hawthorn) to reach the far side at the top. Fortunately we were burgled and the thieves took the hedge-clipper. I hope they are enjoying it. I replaced it with an electric job (19-inch sword, cuts anything up to half an inch with aplomb) and two cables adding up to about 200 feet, enough to reach any of the hedges.

Charmed as I am by by my new hedge-clipper, it has been made intensely clear to me, as an American, that you don't fool around with British electricity. Two hundred and twenty volts is a lot of volts. You use a circuit breaker and try your best not to cut the cable with the hedge-clippers. I have cut two cables so far at £15 each, but the circuit breaker kept me from going up in smoke. My new technique for avoiding this problem involves keeping the cable hanging around the back of my neck while I'm brandishing the clippers. I'd rather strangle myself than be electrocuted.

It was during the same burglary that I lost two other machines: a big American brush-cutter/string trimmer, and a chain saw. Both have since been replaced thanks to my generous insurance underwriter (insurance policies are terrific here compared to American ones, but don't mention the premiums). The gas-powered string trimmer is almost as big as the one I lost, and is capable of cleaning up all of the ragged edges on the property in a single three-hour stint. Of course such a stint leaves me vibrating for the following six hours, and also has a hypnotic effect.

This is encouraged by the sheer efficiency with which the string slices practically anything, including (in addition to grass and weeds) hydrangeas, clematis, and the bark on valuable trees.

Perhaps it is because I feel so close to my machines psychologically that I have had very little trouble making them run. This is not to say that nothing ever goes wrong – who hasn't flooded a mower by choking it before turning on the ignition? – but I have often felt that they make engines better these days, or at least easier to start, than they used to. I have a small blue Australian mower with a two-stroke Japanese engine that is going on 14 years old now, and still starts with scarcely more than a single pull. (You do have to change the sparkplug every third session, but hey, nothing's perfect.) It is important to get the fuel mix right. At the moment I have eight containers lined up in the barn: two mixed 50-to-one with two-stroke oil (for the Australian mower), two mixed 25-to-one (for the chainsaw and the string trimmer) two full of plain unleaded (for the rotovator, the all-terrain mower and two other mowers), and two full of diesel fuel for igniting bonfires. Confusion is possible. I am deeply ashamed to admit that I recently wrecked a chainsaw by mistakenly running it on plain fuel. (In case you're curious about what happened, and don't want to find out for yourself, it ran for twenty-five minutes before irreparably scoring the cylinder head. A brave try on the part of the chainsaw.)

I find I have much more to say about my machines, and no room to say it. This is a pity; I would like to celebrate them all. The all-terrain mower, for example, heroically sinking its blade into a stump. The sober hippopotamus-like rotovator, leaping into the air like a spring colt upon hitting a buried root. The tough new chainsaw jammed, apparently for all time, in the heart of a drooping log. What would I do without them? Gardening would be no fun.

P.S. We have had another burglary. Negotiations with the insurers continue. The burglars left all the hand tools.

Gardening Books

IN 1798 A POLISH TOURIST PAID a visit to Mount Vernon, home of the then-aged George Washington, and was deeply impressed. 'The whole plantation,' he wrote, 'the garden and the rest prove well that a man born with natural taste may guess a beauty without having seen the model. The General has never left America . . . but it seems as if he had copied the best samples of the grand old homesteads of England.' Now it may be that Washington really did have a good eye for landscape design, but it strikes me that M. Niemcewicz was being a bit naïve with his praise. There's not the slightest doubt that Washington, like every other moneyed planter in Virginia (and elsewhere in the newly-formed States), had picked up much of what he knew about gardening and design from books – most likely French and English books.

I don't mean to imply that there's anything disgraceful about this. We all need advice from time to time – some of us more than others, of course. And if poor Washington found himself washed up on the banks of the Potomac with no landscape architect available for a couple of hundred miles, who can blame him for turning to Stephen Switzer or Batty Langley? I'd do the same myself.

In fact I *have* done the same myself. Not, I hasten to say, for instructions on landscape design à la 'Capability' Brown – that way lies more extensive back-hoe work than I'm ready to contemplate – but for answers to more homely mysteries, and for simple amusement. Every August and February, for example, I need to look up how to prune the wisteria. This lovely monster, gradually clawing its way upward over the whole back of the house (and on through the gutters and into the attic) needs, I know, to be pruned in August and February if it is to set blossoms properly. I can remember the months, but for the life of me I can't remember how much I'm supposed to cut off. A book tells me.

I must have at least a hundred gardening books by now, and they tell me lots of things. I haven't counted them lately – they aren't all in one place – but I know they range from the very particular (*Sedums*) to the inanely general (*Floral Fancies*). There are histories like *Plants in Garden History* by Penelope Hobhouse, and pungent how-to miscellanies by Christopher Lloyd, along with reference books (Dorling Kindersley's leviathan door-stops in particular) and books of essays by such favourites as Henry Mitchell. In short, an awful lot of gardening books. Probably, given the bulging condition of my bookshelves, too many.

Books and gardening have been going together for a very long time. The Greek writer Theophrastus was cataloguing plants (in ten volumes, no less) practically as soon as anybody learned to read, and any literate Roman could consult Columella on the best way to tie up grape vines. In the last 400 years the flow has gradually turned into a torrent. In 1891 that great gardener Canon Ellacombe estimated that up to that time more than 10,000 gardening works had been published. The number added since then is almost beyond imagining. So far as I know no one has attempted a census, but whole stores are now devoted to gardening books (there's a good one in London), and even the smallest bookshop seems to boast a shelf or two.

As someone responsible for a few gardening books myself, I occasionally feel a twinge of guilt about this overabundance, but not to the point of giving up writing them, much less reading them. Or, more accurately if shamingly, leafing through them looking at the pictures.

No one with a library of gardening books can be oblivious of the fact that in the past twenty or thirty years pictures have seized the field. It's sad but true that as fine colour printing got better and better, it became harder and harder for publishers and book-buyers alike to resist the allure of all those wildly romantic photographs on temptingly glossy stock. It's just faintly possible that the worm is beginning to turn now – at least I've noticed a few cases where actual words are being printed in a place where a different art director might have inserted yet another picture – but I suspect that gardening glamour, no matter how meretricious, is here to stay. After all, it's pretty difficult for mere prose to match the grandeur of a photograph, in full glowing colour, of a perennial border in high summer, say – especially if the photographer thought to use a sky filter.

It could also be argued – and no doubt is – that pictures tend to be more inspiring than words, and so far as gardening is concerned, inspiration is important, if not crucial. The idea is that the gardener comes upon a sensational spread showing, let us say, a topiary castle complete with crenellations. He is instantly inspired to create his own, from scratch. A thousand words – which, worse luck, need to be read – couldn't hope to stir up the same degree of instant enthusiasm. On the other hand, if he's really going to undertake the job, he'll need to fall back on the words to tell him just how to do it (and how many years it's likely to take him).

So while I admit to enjoying the pictures like a lot of other people, what I really treasure about gardening books are the words. There is some wonderful writing in there (try Katharine White on seed catalogues, or Edward Augustus Bowles on his garden in spring, or Eleanor Perényi on practically anything). While we haven't come to the end of the line with pictures, there's only so much variety available, and the quality of printing cannot be improved upon much more. Perhaps I'm wrong to be pessimistic, but it wouldn't surprise me if publishers suddenly decided that the world simply has as many big pretty picture books as it needs, and called a halt, at least temporarily. In the meantime, there will never be too many brilliantly written books.

And we need the guides. Where else can you go to find out how to garden? Very few of us have a vastly knowledgeable old expert living down the street who can tell us the way to build a cold frame or start pansies from seed. You've got to look it up – and hope that the advice you are getting is good.

This can pose problems. Although I'm American, I happen to live in England and garden in South Wales. Quite a few of my gardening books, including the ones I like best and use most often, are American. Over the years I've become painfully aware that you've got to be careful about gardening like an American in Britain. A case in point is the time I went to an American book for instructions on planting asparagus, only to succeed in drowning the lot. The book said to dig a deep trench, which I obediently and laboriously did. By spring the trench had filled right up to the top with water. The asparagus crowns might as well have been water lilies. I was forced to realize that whereas in America you worry about frost, in sodden South Wales the problem is rain. An English book gave me the straight word: plant asparagus in raised beds for good drainage and forget about the frost.

Sometimes, of course you can't trust a book even though it looks like the right one. I speak now as a writer rather than a reader. For my sins (or rather for money, which some consider to be the same thing), I once got involved in writing captions for a beautifully illustrated gardening manual. We had, I recall, a talented but inflexible art director. Apart from the fact that all art directors have a lot to answer for when it comes to making modern gardening books beautiful but undependable, this man had a particular liking for small pictures laid out sequentially in order to illustrate certain procedures. The captions under the pictures, however, needed to be small too, and – oh agony! – to be precisely squared off.

My assignment was to write captions for a series of eight pictures showing how to make a bonsai tree. Each captions was to be four lines of 36 characters. Exactly. Neither 35 or 37. After labouring most of a night, I did it. It looked fine. It read fine. All the captions squared exactly. I sincerely hope that no one ever tried to make a bonsai tree using my instructions.

So what with one thing and another, I've learned to be circumspect about whose advice I take, and which country it's coming from. Like George Washington, I have a lot to learn, and that includes bonsai trees. George, fortunately, never had one of those little arborial dwarves to worry about, but it does occur to me to wonder about his asparagus patch.

On Keeping Records

A FEW YEARS BACK I WAS HELPING my brother-in-law unpack some cardboard boxes full of books collected for a charity sale in New York State. They didn't amount to much, I have to say – a large contingent of Reader's Digest condensed novels that I wouldn't care to read even if they hadn't been shrunken, some high-school physics textbooks that pre-dated the A-bomb, a mysterious volume or two in what looked like Azerbaijani. But then I noticed a little black leather-bound volume full of clear, tiny handwriting in blue ink. It was, I soon discovered, a garden journal.

I often think of that book and wish I had kept it. I don't know who wrote it, but I suspect it was a woman because of the handwriting and the precision with which the entries were made. (Sorry if that sounds sexist, but that's what I thought at the time, and still do.) It recorded the usual things: the weather (particularly frosts), dates when significant garden events took place (the first early potatoes, new peas, lilac bloom), the names of flowers and vegetables planted. It also made note of chores that needed to be done and ideas for improving the garden, as well as comments on how some previous plans had turned out. The little book was clearly a labour of love, compiled with care and attention over at least forty years by someone whose garden represented an important part of her life.

One thing, however, made this garden diary different from a thousand others: it had been tossed out with the trash. This could only mean that the author had died. The chain had been broken. The fact that yellow tulips opened on 12 May in 1967 in Cropseyville was no longer of any interest to anybody at all, while the prospects for the new perennial bed behind the garage (new in 1958, that is) were, frankly, nil.

I still find this mildly poignant, but it does serve to point up the transience of gardens (to say nothing of that of human life). What it does *not* do is to suggest that garden books and diaries are in any way a waste of time, just because the author may be the only reader. Keeping track of what goes where (or, in far too many cases, went), noting successes and failures, setting down the details of purchases, sowings, harvests and whatnot, and generally compiling some sort of permanent record of this most impermanent creation may not be essential, but it's fun, and it may even have some practical value. I say this in the full awareness of my own failings as a record-keeper, of which I received a painful reminder the other day.

A year ago we made a new border out of a section of lawn overhung by lilacs and occupied by clumps of blind daffodils. It is big – 15 feet wide and more than 50 feet long – and as I was the one who wanted it, it fell to me to fill it up. This I did in my habitual disorganized way. I moved some plants from other beds – a couple of parahebes, half a dozen veronica plants, two or three buddleias, a couple of flowering currants, a batch of red and white penstemons Carol had started from cuttings, a large autumn-flowering 'Herbstfreude' sedum, which I split up into pieces, a smoke bush, one or two roses. Then I bought some more: a pretty little horizontal *Cornus controversa*, erigerons, *Coreopsis verticillata* 'Moonbeam', a *Thalictrum aquilegiifolium*, and four dahlias – two 'Bishop of Llandaff', a 'Small World', and a 'Moor Place'. Finally, I started an unfeasible quantity of annuals from seed: flax, white cosmos, *Nicotiana sylvestris*, and what turned out to be entirely too much *Limnanthes*, sowed around the corners of the bed.

Last summer the border performed well, apart from some obvious overcrowding in places (the cosmos fell down on the dahlias, the nicotiana fell down on the penstemons, the flax simply fell down) and a few gaps where nothing took. In the autumn I cut away everything that looked dead and tossed compost wherever I could see bare earth. All was well and good during the winter, but then spring arrived.

The problem immediately presenting itself was that while the shrubs were easy enough to see, the perennials had mostly vanished. They were there somewhere, I was sure, submerged beneath a scattering of compost, chickweed and baby nettles; certain unidentifiable leafy clusters might actually be plants I wanted, rather than weeds. It was at this point that I remembered a clumsy sketch of the bed I had made last summer, hunted for it, and found it wedged in a jacket pocket. No map was ever more welcome to a lost traveller. The sketch allowed me to dig over the bed with reasonable confidence that I wasn't doing any actual harm. I even rediscovered – and preserved – a few late emergers (a clump of the *Coreopsis verticillata*, for example) that I was sure had expired in the January freeze.

Now to anyone serious about garden journals and record-keeping, this must seem just a tad pathetic. Christopher Lloyd has said somewhere that you shouldn't even visit a new garden without a notebook in hand, and surely he is living proof of the wisdom of keeping track of what your own plants are doing, or not doing, under varying conditions. There may be people who can keep it all in their heads, but most of us are human. Besides, a garden journal can be, in its own modest way, a work of art, or at least something more than one of those places where facts accumulate like dead leaves in a clogged gutter.

One of the greatest of garden diarists was the eighteenth-century naturalist Gilbert White, rector of Selborne in Hampshire, who for twenty years recorded everything from the price of manure to the vicissitudes of his 'cantaleupes' in his *Garden-Kalendar*. (He seems to have picked up the habit from his brother-in-law, a man with a reputation for 'extreme Abstractedness and Speculativeness', who for no less than seventy years kept a record of each day's weather.) More than most garden diaries, White's can actually be read with interest if not pleasure; it tells a great deal about gardening practice 250 years ago, and frequently goes beyond dry dates and numbers to deliver such curious facts as the need for ageing melon seeds before planting. (If you don't have time to age them properly, you should carry them in your breeches pocket for two months.) That White was an obsessive watcher and note-taker will be obvious to anyone who has read his classic *Natural History of Selborne*; his garden diary, which anticipated it, shares some of the same charm.

Gilbert White's writings are a fine example of the way attention to minutiae can create something of lasting value. Needless to say, this doesn't always – or often – happen. As a rule garden diaries are addressed mostly to the writer himself or herself. Thomas Jefferson's

Garden Book, occupied as it largely is with notes on the weather, will never have the readership of the Declaration of Independence. Still, as Henry Mitchell in *The Essential Earthman* points out, 'a gardener profits from small trifling facts, and the more of them he has observed, the more resonant, the richer, his enjoyment becomes. . . . It is not the fact that is important, but the gardener's awareness that a fact is being beheld.'

I find this a very convincing argument in favour of even the most pedestrian kind of record-keeping. It goes right back to the spirit of the eighteenth-century clergyman keeping a weather diary in hopes of detecting something of God's will in a yearly pattern of hailstorms and early frosts. To know, as Henry Mitchell describes doing thanks to his garden book, that his daylily 'Lady Bountiful' ('which is old and not very worthwhile') had begun blooming on 16 May two years running made its next date of bloom a matter of exceptional interest. Any garden is rich in such potential epiphanies.

In the end, though, we have to come back to the practical value of keeping garden records. I'm delighted to report that in spite of my laziness there is hope in this quarter for the garden of Towerhill Cottage. A short while ago Carol began building a really splendid garden journal in the chips and synapses of her laptop computer. Each month has a file to itself, with a week-by-week summary of jobs to be done (and completed), the weather, plant purchases, notes on what has flowered, and so on. April alone has more than three pages, heavily job-laden (January is of course skimpier). Then she has created a plant list giving the names of a considerable number of the flowers, shrubs and vegetables we have incorporated in the garden so far, along with their location and – sometimes – their fate ('10 *Corydalis solida* in pot in barn; all eaten by mice'). She has even begun entering information about each plant from reference books and catalogues. This has already come in handy in a slightly unusual way. Last fall, expecting a crop of nice smooth oval 'Belle de Fontenay' potatoes, I was horrified to discover a lot of bumpy contorted red objects that appeared to have undergone some monstrous mutation. The cyberfile revealed that I had actually planted 'Pink Fir Apple'. Intense relief.

As far as I can see, the only things lacking in our newfangled garden journal are diagrams showing exactly where such precious objects as that *Coreopsis verticillata* may be found lurking in early spring. So far, however, we haven't figured out how to make the computer co-operate in this. The result is scrappy pieces of paper all around the place. Possibly the answer is a small leather-bound book.

Topiary

CONSIDERED OBJECTIVELY, the idea of whittling large green things out of what would otherwise be shapeless trees is bizarre in the extreme. Yet that's what topiary is all about. Do you fancy a toadstool ten feet in diameter? How about a monster teapot? A corkscrew fit for an entire hogshead of wine? Or possibly nothing more than a gargantuan verdant chicken? Well, take a yew and start clipping.

It is easy, unavoidable almost, to be frivolous about topiary, especially in its remoter reaches where it consorts with garden gnomes and upended bathtubs transformed into religious shrines. Probably no other gardening practice has had such a chequered career, from admiration to obloquy and back again. Four hundred years ago Sir Francis Bacon was declaring that 'I for my part do not like images cut in juniper or other garden stuff; they be for children' (though he rather liked a 'well-clippt' hedge), while much nearer our own time the great William Robinson likened it to 'the cramming of Chinese feet into impossible shoes'.

Often attacks on topiary were really attacks on something else – on formal gardens as opposed to naturalistic plantings, on closed-in garden 'rooms' as opposed to the grand sweep of lawns, on labour-intensive gardening as opposed to low maintenance. Yet it has never been quite without supporters. In spite of the savagely funny put-down by Alexander Pope in his 'Catalogue of Greens', in spite of the bulldozer tactics of the eighteenth-century landscape designers, in spite of the marked shortage these days of happy though underpaid artists with hedge-clippers, topiary is still with us. We may even be in the midst of a modest topiary boom.

The principal reason for suggesting this is the current fashion for dividing up the garden and defining its structure by means of hedges. Topiary, after all, encompasses hedges of all sorts, from the simple, solid and rectilinear through those featuring spherical or pyramidal finials to the most complicated and beswagged decorative 'walls'. From the latter, of course, it's not a giant leap to other kinds of 'vegetable sculpture', if your taste runs that way.

While English cottage gardens have always featured bits of topiary, it was the so-called 'old-fashioned garden' movement of the last part of the nineteenth-century that brought it strongly to the fore again. This style called for 'architectural' hedging featuring niches and archways, and plenty of low box borders surrounding billows of 'cottagey' flowers – sunflowers, lilies, poppies, daisies. Such cultural pace-setters as the poet Dante Gabriel Rossetti and the designer-writer William Morris were charmed by topiary. On holiday in Sussex in 1866, Rossetti found a complete topiary armchair in a country garden, contrived to buy it, and transplanted it to the Pre-Raphaelite precincts of Cheyne Walk in London, where it promptly died. Morris had better luck with his yew dragon at Kelmscott Manor. He named it Fafnir and for years held a formal dragon-trimming ceremony, setting about it (as his biographer Fiona MacCarthy notes) 'with large shears', According to Brent Elliott, the author of *Victorian Gardens*, the popularity of this sort of figurative topiary with the general public was largely the work of nurserymen who imported finished specimens from Holland, one of whom rejoiced in the name Herbert J. Cutbush and used to exhibit 'Cutbush's Cut Bushes' at flower shows around the country.

Because yew lives so long – an 800-year-old tree in a village churchyard is a commonplace; we've got one leaning over the wall outside St Bridget's down in Skenfrith – an unspoken assumption is that all topiary must be enormously old. Age is one of its attractions. Various examples of venerable topiary in England, like the great display at Levens Hall in Cumbria, have achieved the reputation of being practically medieval. This isn't necessarily true. Elliott points out that although Levens, for example, was first laid out about 1700, upkeep of the great yew figures lapsed, and much of what's there now – looking authentically ancient, I have to say – probably dates back no further than 175 years or so. That's still pretty old, but hardly ageless.

Given its reputation for slow growth, gardening with yew is an intimidating business. You can have a fine magnolia in two or three years, and even a laggard wisteria is going to look substantial before much more time than that has passed, but yew? Who's got 800 years (or even 175) to wait? There's no getting around the fact that yew is *the* tree for topiary – dark rich green, close-needled, easy to clip – at least in Britain where the climate favours it. Box, a close second, is no more forward.

I've been reading a little book suggesting that whatever one's opinion of the result may be, undertaking topiary is not necessarily an activity requiring two or three lifetimes to complete. The book is a reprint of Nathaniel Lloyd's *Garden Craftsmanship in Yew and Box*, first published in 1925, with an introduction by the author's famous gardening offspring Christopher Lloyd. A practical handbook to planting, cultivating, and shaping the raw materials of topiary, its original publication gave a boost to a fashion that had been growing since the 1880s. (It also, incidentally, stimulated a typically explosive comment from William Robinson, beginning 'It is the poorest book that so far has disgraced the garden.' Robinson had his own agenda, and it most definitely did not include topiary.)

Lloyd's main point, which he illustrates with frequent reference to his own garden at Great Dixter, is that for ornamental hedging the common yew, *Taxus baccata*, is not only superior to all other trees and bushes, deciduous and evergreen alike, but 'is actually one of the quickest growing of all hedge plants, and no other responds so well to suitable treatment'. (Box is indeed slower, but has the special virtue of needing to be clipped less often, and is especially good for miniature hedges.) The key is to choose the right sort of infant stock, and then to plant the little trees in the proper conditions. No point in thinking about green peacocks at this stage.

According to experiments he conducted, Lloyd argues that the quickest results come from setting out relatively small pyramidal plants, well branched at the bottom, in double-dug, well-drained soil enriched with thoroughly-rotted manure. Three-foot specimens proved to mature fastest. Pillar-shaped yews took much longer to fill in at the base, and between a third and a half of the 4½- and 6-foot plants simply died. One new hedge of 3-footers, regularly and tightly clipped, reached a height of no less than 8 feet in twelve years, with a base

5½ feet wide! Even more remarkable was Lloyd's experience with tiny 1-foot plants, which took longer to start looking like a hedge but caught up with the 3-footers in about ten years.

Clipping, according to Lloyd, should be undertaken in early autumn because growth has then virtually stopped and everything will look sharp and tidy for eight or nine months. A hedge should be cut with a batter – sloping sides – which keeps the lower parts from being starved of light. And if radical cutting is required to restore the batter, or because your yew has been allowed to get out of hand, don't worry; it can stand it.

This latter point struck me as particularly pertinent. In the last few weeks we have visited several gardens where serious surgery on old yews had been undertaken. At Powys Castle in North Wales, a very old yew hedge had been sliced back to the main trunks along its whole length earlier in the summer; two or three months later you could already see the new growth beginning to emerge. The same was true at Hortus editor David Wheeler's garden in Herefordshire, where a ninety-year-old yew hedge had to be truncated to permit a new garden plan. Frankly I wouldn't have given this bit of hackwork much chance of recovering, but I'm now sure it will. The other example is in my own garden, where a six-foot wide cylinder of yew makes up part of a mixed hedge otherwise consisting of hazel, privet, hawthorn, elder, dog rose and stinging nettles. The entire top of this was inadvertently sheared off a couple of years ago by the flail mower that does farm hedges. Within six months it was sprouting nicely, and now boasts an entirely plausible yew dove (or possibly turkey – you decide) squatting on top.

It was the discovery of this chunk of yew, combined with Lloyd's chapter on 'Topiary Specimen Trees,' that inspired me to think that I could (before I was too old to care anymore) create something a little more complicated and interesting than a hedge. As Lloyd says, when 'treated with restraint, such clipped trees . . . provide a certain atmosphere'. This may not be true of, say, a rabbit, but a turtle, has a certain charm, and a bird is entirely appropriate. Lloyd, in fact, observes that 'forming birds . . . is so easily done that any intelligent person can undertake them'. He also points out that there is no reason why you can't start with something simple like a cone with a button top and let it grow into a coffee pot or a peacock, rather like carving something out of stone, only backwards.

In his introduction to his father's book, Christopher Lloyd advises the novice to 'aim for broad effect and don't try to be too elaborate or clever'. This strikes me as wise. Anyhow, my bird apart, the most affecting topiary may not be the yew man on the yew horse chasing a yew fox with a yew hound (which we saw yesterday, looking a bit the worse for wear, at Usk Castle House garden) but the black-green bulk of a sheared yew hedge backed by the bare branches of a winter tree against a white winter sky. I'm moved by the very thought of it.

Old Saws

I've NEVER LIVED IN A PLACE where people were so concerned about the weather. This is probably the result of never knowing quite what to expect. In America, especially on the East Coast, predictions are pretty dependable; after all, the weather systems have a whole continent to cross (and be examined *en route*) before they fall upon you. Mistakes occur, of course, but not big ones, and not all that often.

In England, on the other hand, we have to take what we often unexpectedly get. The Met Office has gingerly begun offering five-day forecasts, but in my experience they are fairly useless; presumably only so many sources of information are floating around out there on the Atlantic, and the weather satellites have apparent limitations. Longer range forecasts – that it will be an 'iron' winter, say, or that we should expect a drought in three months time – are hardly worth bothering about.

In the past, of course, the English lacked even the Met Office to tell them about visibility off Rockall or the likelihood of rain in Suffolk by dawn on Wednesday. What they had instead was a vast and baroque system of folk knowledge about the weather, incorporated in axioms and sayings of splendid inconsistency. Americans will recognize some of them – 'Red sky in the morning, shepherd's warning', or 'If March comes in like a lion, it will go out like a lamb', both of which are, incidentally, true more often than not. No doubt they were exported to the United States centuries ago along with the sack of barley seed and the bundle of apple cuttings. But a lot of others are purely English, possibly because they definitely won't work anywhere else. In lieu of ironclad guarantees from the Met Office, they're still filling in the gaps.

My own favourite source of weather wisdom is Uncle Offa. Each month he produces a column in the *Monmouthshire Beacon and Forest of Dean Gazette*, our local paper, in which he sets forth what we've got to look forward to during the weeks ahead. Offa (in fact a retired army major named Frederick Hingston, who lives a few miles from Monmouth up on the Trellech Ridge) seems to know every old saw, saying, prognosticatory trick and significant saint's day in the book. He also displays a satisfying lack of gullibility – real discrimination, in fact – about the dependability of what he's purveying.

The only problem is that most of these ancient insights were developed by farmers, for farmers. Gardeners may find them less useful. A year or two ago, for instance, Offa offered us half a dozen traditional views on May weather and its consequences. Some seemed to agree: 'Rain in May brings bread throughout the year' jibes with 'A leaky May and a dry June, puts the harvest right in tune'. But then ther is: 'A dry May foretells a wholesome year' and 'A wet May spells a dry September'. All, as he remarks, very confusing. For what it's worth I recall that it did rain quite a bit in May and now, in September (after a drought-ridden summer), the rains are beginning again. Offa admits that May is the most difficult month in the year for the soothsayer.

Probably the best-known long-range forecasting day in Britain is St Swithin's Day, 15 July. Offa reckons that about half the population believes the rhyme tied to it:

> St Swithin's Day if thou dost rain
> Full forty days it will remain,
> St. Swithin's Day if thou art fair
> Full forty days 'twill rain nae mair.

The eighteenth-century poet John Gay went along with it when he memorably rewrote the first two lines in *Trivia*:

> If on St Swithin's feast the welkin lours,
> And every pent house streams with showers,
> Twice twenty days shall clouds their fleeces drain
> And wash the pavement with incessant rain.

Judging from the weather that followed our rainless St Swithin's this summer, when we all thought it would 'rain nae mair', this one seems to have some logic behind it.

Still, there is something rather helpless about long-range predictions like these. Pointed suggestions that you are in for a bad year is cold comfort to us modern gardeners, and an old-time farmer doomed to a rainy haymaking a couple of months hence might well be inclined to give up the whole show and emigrate. Fortunately, for more practical purposes there is traditional counsel on such things as when to expect a late frost, how and when to do your planting, and the kind of weather you might be handed tomorrow morning, rather than a season or two later.

I confess to being slightly baffled by Offa's May planting advice, which is specific in terms of dates, but based on the signs of the zodiac, which I've never understood. Anyhow, he says you are supposed to plant 'above ground crops' in Taurus (May 1), Cancer (May 5–6), or Libra (May 12–13). Root crops should be sowed during Scorpio (May 14–15), or Capricorn (May 18–19). Another source, however, points out that 'Beans should blow before May doth go', which doesn't leave much time. It also observes: 'Sow beans in mud, they'll grow like wood.' This, I know from bitter experience, is true, but my garden is seldom dry enough (or warm enough) for beans before June. As a totally confusing clincher, we have 'Who sows in May gets little that way', which I suppose has to be interpreted to mean that May is too late.

Other planting instructions are a bit sounder, including this one in favour of putting out saplings in autumn: 'Apples, pears, hawthorn, quick, oak; set them at All-Hallows-Tide [November 1] and command them to prosper; set them at Candlemas [February 2] and entreat them to grow.' No less sensible is 'This rule in gardening never forget, To sow dry and set wet.'

On the frost front, we've got 'A mist in March is a frost in May', and 'So many fogs in March, so many frosts in May', both of which strike me as overly pessimistic. But Blackthorn Winter – April 11 to 14 – is plausible: 'Just as the blackthorn is coming into blossom, expect a cold snap.' If blackthorn puts out blossoms before the leaves appear, says Offa, watch out even more carefully for a bitter spell. Indeed our *Magnolia* x *soulangeana* took a beating at exactly that time this spring, though I can't tell you whether blossoms or leaves came first on the blackthorn.

Husbandry

The behaviour of trees and other plants as a device for predicting weather or choosing planting times has a long and relatively respectable history. According to Eleanor Perényi, it even has a scientific-sounding name, 'phenology'. Actually, that term covers all kinds of 'naturally recurring phenomena, esp. in relation to climatic conditions' (to quote the *Concise Oxford English Dictionary*), so the thickness of the fur on a woolly bear caterpillar as advance notice of a hard winter is just as phenological as keeping an eye on a so-called 'indicator plant'. Nevertheless, it is easier to accept the word of a plant, so to speak. Lilac buds, for instance, tend not to open until after the last frost, and such timing ties in with other natural events. Perényi tells how farmers in Montana know that when the lilac blooms they have ten days to make a cut of alfalfa and eliminate the first brood of alfalfa weevils. Oak trees are exceptionally weather-sensitive organisms, if you believe the folk sayings. In New England, when the oak leaves are the size of a mouse's ear, you go out looking for morels (I did this without luck for years, and still don't whether to blame the oaks or the morels). Over here oak leaves of that size are supposed to indicate that the ground is warm enough for seeds to germinate.

Perényi is firmly convinced that gardeners ought to pay more attention to this kind of thing, and it does make sense. I'm less convinced that plants have much to tell us – unambiguously – about short-term weather prospects. The oak v. ash observations are a case in point. One classic saying goes: 'Oak before ash, sign of a splash; ash before oak, sign of a soak.' Translated, this seems to mean that if the oak puts on leaves before the ash, there will be a quick shower and little more, but if the ash leafs first, there will be extended heavy rains. But what do we do about this: 'If the ash before the oak comes out, There has been, or will be, a drought'?

Is the behaviour of other plants any more trustworthy? English tradition says that when goatsbeard (*Tragopogon pratensis*, otherwise known as Johnny-go-to-bed-at-noon) closes up before midday, there is rain in the air; if the petals stay open, the weather is set fair. If you see clover leaves closed and pointing to the sky, 'reach for your brolly'. And Welsh poppies and rock roses drooping also mean rain. Frankly, much as I would like to be in tune with the cosmos, nosing around the undergrowth to find out whether it is a day for puttying the windows or for staying inside tying flies is just too much trouble. In this case, I'll go with the Met Office.

There remains the question of just how much of this stuff is folk wisdom, and how much is a good rhyme. Oddly, the more apocalyptic sayings seem to reflect experience at least as well, or better, than the trivial ones. Offa reports hearing this one in Devon: 'If St Paul's Day [January 25] be fine, expect a good harvest. If it is wet or snowy expect a famine. If it is windy, expect a war.' That has the weary ring of authenticity. On the other hand, 'When eager bites the thirsty flea, clouds and rain you'll surely see' hardly washes. I'm tempted to make up my own about then – or at least to stay tuned to Radio 4 for the 6:57 forecast.

Design and its Discontents

To LOOK AT IT, YOU WOULD never have guessed that the garden represented anything but absolute calm. A couple of placid pools flanked by stone and shaved grass, some long shallow steps, a clutch of hedges, and what the judges praised as 'restrained herbaceous borders' when they gave it a Gold Medal and named it the overall best garden at the RHS's Chelsea Flower Show in 1998. It is, in fact, the very model of a modern English garden, as elegant as Lady Arabella Lennox-Boyd herself, who designed it.

Or did she? This is the question that has been exercising the gardening cognoscenti ever since the last gallon of clear water filled the pools precisely to overflowing and the last water lily was fixed delicately in place. The problem is that some twenty years ago, the well-known Belgian designer Jacques Wirtz designed a garden that closely – altogether too closely, some say – resembles Lady Arabella's. What's more, Wirtz's garden is famous, having appeared in several books, and is regarded as a classic of the designer's art.

Like a hurricane in a frog pond, the affair splashed mud in all directions. As soon as he heard about it, Wirtz, furious, dispatched a letter to the RHS pointing out the similarities and demanding that the award be withdrawn. Defending his judges, RHS director general Gordon Rae (who has since retired) declared stoutly that the Lennox-Boyd garden 'clearly deserved its Gold Medal' and described the dispute as 'regrettable'. Meanwhile another Wirtz letter, claiming breach of intellectual rights, rocketed off to Lady Arabella, who refused to comment. Her lawyers simply denied the allegations and argued that the garden no longer existed anyway. This was of course true – like all Chelsea show gardens, it had been pulled up and carted away at the close of festivities.

It remains unclear just how the dispute will be resolved, if indeed it ever is. According to Wirtz's lawyer, no legal action had been initiated as of six months after the show, although, in the classic phrase, 'we are keeping our options open'. These presumably include going ahead with the threat, made earlier, to 'sue for breach of copyright under the Berne Convention.' But can a garden be copyrighted? Quite apart from the matter of whose pool is more original, which I am wholly unqualified to adjudicate, I find this question a fascinating one.

As a former publisher, I've always been interested in plagiarism. There's plenty of it around to contend with, starting in college if not before. I note that researchers at Birmingham University recently announced the development of a clever computer program that is supposed to be able to identify, at the touch of a button, an essay copied from a friend or purchased from the Internet by a over-stressed student. On a more serious level – that is, in court – cases of straight textual piracy turn up with some frequency. And then there are the oddities that give rise to argument, legal and otherwise. Last year the New York publisher Farrar, Straus & Giroux gave up an attempt to publish a sequel to Vladimir Nabokov's novel *Lolita*, under pressure from the author's estate. Written in the form of Lolita's own diary, the book was dismissed by Nabokov lawyers as a 'rip-off' of the original. To date, however, nobody has ever successfully maintained copyright in a fictional character. 'From a lawyer's point of view,' remarked publisher Roger Straus wearily, 'it would have been a delicious case.'

No doubt the case of Wirtz v. Lennox-Boyd would be equally delicious (from the lawyers' point of view, that is), because so far as I can discover nobody has ever attempted to establish a copyright on a garden, either. Geert Glas, the Belgian attorney who represents Wirtz, feels strongly that this should be possible. 'I don't see why you can protect the design of a house, or the text of a book, or a painting or an opera or choreography – but not a garden. It is after all the expression of an idea. Even if an idea cannot be copyrighted, the unique expression of that idea should be.'

There is a certain healthy logic to Glas's position, but making a test case out of Jacques Wirtz could prove awkward. Few gardener designers have been as influential – i.e. as much copied and imitated – as he. His style is distinctive, relying heavily on box, beech, yew and hornbeam to establish strong architectural lines and create avenues of trees and hedges. He likes to introduce private sheltered corners, and to retain a human scale even in the grandest constructions.

Jcques Wirtz would probably be among the first to admit that garden designers draw on their predecessors for ideas. Similarly, a spokeswoman in Lady Arabella's office notes that she too 'gets her inspiration from many sources'. But inspiration is not the same thing as copying, and this where the affair of the Chelsea gold medal water garden gets interesting. As a London legal expert points out, 'Copyright exists in the most trivial things. Why not a garden? Simply putting pencil to paper establishes it; you don't have to register it. And it would be a very odd garden indeed that didn't have some written record behind it, some notes or sketches. It's easy to say that there are only so many plants and so many ways to design a garden, but that's like saying there are only twenty-six letters in the alphabet.' He thinks Wirtz could sue, and might very well win, although making a claim stick could be very complicated.

Are there any lessons here for the rest of us, assiduously garden-visiting and storing up ideas to be used in our own unprofessional endeavours? Christopher Lloyd has always maintained that ideas are there for the taking (though he might not put it that way), and regards keeping one's eyes and notebook open as essential. Few of us are brave or knowledgeable enough to ignore the advice of books and magazines, and the urge to emulate is never far behind a surge of admiration. For the time being, though, it might be advisable to hold off building that water garden with the rectangular pools, shaved grass, hedges, and 'restrained herbaceous borders'. In any event, don't go for the gold.

The modern garden, like modern music, is still not much loved. Most of us are suckers for a good tune or, to put it another way, for a Jekyllian perennial border full of flowers, an evocative drift of spring bulbs, or even the colourful jumble of a cottage garden. The problem is that modern garden design seems determined to deny us these pleasures, without offering much in their place except cement. At least that what I thought, before discovering the work of Jacques Wirtz.

Now in his seventies, Wirtz has quietly achieved a position of extraordinary influence. His gardens are in a distinctly modern idiom, yet warm and humane, never arid or difficult. Most of his career was spent working for private clients in the area around his native Antwerp; today his name is being mentioned in the same breath with Le Nôtre or Capability Brown. In the last decade his commissions have ranged from gardens for Valentino and Catherine Deneuve to the Tuileries Gardens in Paris; he is currently engaged in designing the grounds of a ducal castle in Northumberland; and will soon begin work on his first gardens in the United States. In the world of modern garden design, Jacques Wirtz is fascinating – and redeeming – figure.

Early one morning (he starts early), I called on Wirtz in Schoten, the Antwerp suburb where he has his home. We met in one of his office buildings, long, low wood structures with lots of glass that replaced the too-small original studios in the stables next to the house a year or two ago. His son Martin, who with his brother Peter works with his father, joined us. Dressed in a yellow v-neck sweater and a sports shirt, Jacques Wirtz looked more like a man ready for eighteen holes at Pebble Beach than a *paysagiste*, but the seriousness with which he spoke about his work soon erased that impression.

I hesitantly mentioned the Chelsea contretemps and he admitted to being annoyed; the affair had touched a nerve. But in fact 80 per cent of all the new gardens in Belgium have been influenced by his work. The most marked influence, without question, is the use of hedges. Wirtz is famous for his hedges, which he began introducing into his gardens forty years ago, at a time when the whole tradition of topiary and 'green architecture' was virtually obsolete, and old hedges were being destroyed. He was attracted by the structural strength they could give, not only in the form of boundary walls but also inside the garden, to form axes, perspective lines and curtains. Most of the hundred-plus gardens he has created in his lifetime do feature hedges – hornbeam, beech, box, yew – although he employs other materials too, and some his most successful designs make use of great mounds of such grasses as *Pennisetum*, *Miscanthus* and *Stipa*. Part of the reason the hedges have received so much attention, he suspects, is because they are so photogenic. What he really likes is mass, whether in shrubs or grasses or hedging – so long as they are not 'little heaps of plants'. And he has no objection to obscuring the house, especially if he doesn't like the architecture. 'Clients cannot imagine that I can do this, but you rarely find a truly interesting house.'

Wirtz grew up in Antwerp, the son of a broker. His summers were spent in the country, and this exposure to nature clearly meant a lot to him. He claims to have been poor student ('like many geniuses', he jokes) but came into his stride when he entered a three-year course at a horticultural college. The training was severe ('like the army') and concentrated on horticulture and botany – almost no landscape design. He approves of this balance; too many students concentrate on the design and fail to learn enough about plants. Graduating soon after the end of the War, he started a small business growing flowers for cutting, then contemplated starting a nursery. It was not until 1950 that he designed his first complete garden. He had to struggle to get commissions. 'I would take my little truck, drive round looking for houses being built and ring doorbells.' The jobs – and his reputation – gradually increased.

Today, with more and bigger commissions rolling in all the time, especially since 1990 when he won a competition to redesign the Carrousel Garden in Paris, Wirtz is lucky to have two of his sons to work with him. 'They grew up in a garden,' he says, 'they had no choice.' In fact, they have both had the kind of training Wirtz believes in – for Martin, university in Ghent, followed by a year working with the noted plantsman Michael Hickson at Knightshayes Garden Trust in Devon; for Peter, a degree in horticulture from Cornell University. It is clear that they share Wirtz's vision of what a garden should be – a precise, emotionally affecting demonstration of tension between control and spontaneity.

Wirtz's own garden at Botermelk ('Buttermilk'), while less 'designed' than many of the gardens he has created from scratch, is a singularly beautiful illustration of his approach. Martin Wirtz took me through it as patches of sun followed by brisk showers moved swiftly across the lawns and hedges.

Wirtz bought Botermelk, once the home of the head gardener at a baron's castle nearby, thirty-odd years ago. More or less lost in a forest of huge old trees, with five or six acres of grounds hopelessly overgrown after decades of abandonment, it boasted a few dozen ancient fruit trees, a bit of cow pasture, some chicken runs, a collapsed greenhouse (victim of a German buzz-bomb in 1945), and mountainous box hedges still vaguely marking out the borders of the walks that cut the garden into four main blocks. The temptation must have been great to clean everything out and start over, but Wirtz had the prescience to see past the ruin to what the garden had been, and what, given his creative eye, it could become.

Today, from the moment you park beneath a massive crenellated wall of clipped hornbeam, it is the hedges you notice about Botermelk. Hedges of low *Buxus microphylla* var. *japonica* bordering the walk around the house, severely squared box hedges edging the immaculate lawns and walks, and above all the huge billowing masses of the old original overgrown box, now brought under control like so many green cumulus clouds tethered to earth. To produce these, Martin explained, it took ten years of careful pruning and shaping, and then another five years before the last holes filled in. Box cannot be hurried. But the result is spectacular. One huge irregular mound crouches next to the house, others line the paths crossing the main garden sections, yet there is never any sense of crowding or enclosure; these are hedges miraculously transformed into abstractions, into green sculpture.

Unlikely as it may seem, Botermelk is both a working garden and a place to enjoy. Each of the four main blocks is filled with specimen plants and trees that may well be moved out someday to take a place in a newly-designed Wirtz garden elsewhere. There are beds filled with a huge variety of topiary box and yew, perennial beds (when I was there, several hundred identical dark blue delphiniums rose regimentally above a bordering hedge), trees, roses and many young or extra-large shrubs, some rare – viburnums, styrax, halesia, magnolias, azaleas and rhododendrons. Even the pleasure garden, a tightly-hedged small formal enclosure crammed with dozens of perennials from phlox to thalictrum to euphorbias – and of course roses – is in fact a *proeftuin* ('test-garden') where the Wirtzes try out new varieties. (Most Wirtz gardens, incidentally, include a flower garden, though it may be placed at a distance from the house and is often hedged. Despite the fame of his hedges, he has a passion for flowering plants.) Scattered across the open beds are aged fruit trees. They will of course stay, as will many of the trees, shrubs and topiary that have become too old and beautiful to give up.

In case this sounds like some kind of cobbled-together nursery, be assured that it isn't. The precision with which Jacques Wirtz has calculated the alignment and effect of the hedges, old and new, the contrast between the ebullience of the plantings and the formality of the design, the severe horizontality of the lawns and the spaciousness of the setting, has created a most seductive feeling of combined calm and tension. It may not be an absolutely typical Wirtz garden – there probably isn't such a thing, given his willingness to make use of such a wide range of structural materials (hedges, grasses, trees, even stone blocks), water and lawns. His most famous designs are extremely simple – for example the garden at Hasselt, reincarnated at Chelsea, which consists mainly of hedging, a square stone-flanked pool, and some steps. Or the bluestone pyramids planted among great trees in a park near Botermelk. Or the use of ivy as rolling groundcover, out of which rise groves of flowering cherries and native trees on the University of Antwerp campus.

A French critic has spoken of Wirtz's 'permanent dialogue with natural environment', and that really isn't too fancy a way to put it. In his work, nature is never silenced, but goes right on talking to us, in a way so engaging and fascinating that even the most confirmed cottage gardener could become a convert. Yet there is no question, in any of his gardens, who is in charge. I find this hugely exciting. Although I still have my doubts about modern music, if this is where modern garden design is going, I say terrific.

Names

IT CAME AS SOMETHING OF A SURPRISE to me the other day to
realize that, without really trying to, I've picked up a lot of Latin
plant names. My collection can't compare with the horticultural
vocabulary of serious gardeners, botanists and other taxonomy
experts, but I've begun to get a grip on some of the meanings, which
makes the names easier to remember. If I could now only remember the
common names to go with them, and even better, to identify plants
growing in the garden, I'd be on the way to a useful kind of fluency.
Still, you've got to start somewhere.

Gardeners, I've found, really do care about names. Even readers of
the august Royal Horticultural Society journal *The Garden*, whose
sophistication might have been expected to accomodate such matters,
have been writing in to complain about the violence being done to old
familiars. In view of the fact that the world of plants is such a
multifarious and unsettled place, this is understandable. Names impose
a comforting sense of order and it's all the more shocking, therefore,
when they are officially changed. A *Chrysanthemum* becomes a
Dendranthema and the world wobbles on its axis.

What we have to accept, of course, that if the names *weren't*
changed in accord with new knowledge, or in some way organized in
a scientifically logical fashion, we would all be in a still more serious
state of disarray. 'The especial vice of *Campanula* is a vanity that leads
to a perfectly appalling plurality of epithets,' the rock plant specialist
Reginald Farrer observed in his usual pointed way in 1920. 'Every
species has about half a dozen different titles, and it is thus that such
confusion reigns in gardens and catalogues – each grower choosing the
name he likes best, until no one knows what his plant really, definitely,
finally is, but wallows in a hopeless muddle from which the only escape
is to buy every mortal *Campanula* you see advertized.' Saxifrages were

no better. And even this was an improvement over the time when Linnaeus, the eighteenth-century Swedish inventor of the system of Latin binomials we all depend on (genus name followed by species name followed by – if necessary – a sub-species name and/or a cultivar name), could attack an earlier naming system as 'a mere confusion of chaos, whose mother was barbarity, whose father dogmatism, whose nurse prejudice.' Scholars can get emotional too.

Gardeners have had to face the problem of calling old plant friends by new names for a long time, and have been complaining about it for just as long. The great gardener William Robinson, a notably crochety fellow, conducted a running battle with Kew over its insistence on using Latin plant names in preference to Robinson's sometimes bizarre English ones. In rather the same spirit (but with no more success), poet and garden writer Geoffrey Grigson argued against the raging tide of Latin equivalents, which were often, as he put it, 'like sand or burrs in the mouth'. No one, he claimed, could 'go about mouthing araucaria, kniphofia (or even tritoma), datura, yucca, dielytra or dicentra.' Grigson wrote that forty years ago; I don't find it difficult to go round mouthing them today. In fact I get a superior feeling doing so.

It is certainly possible to find fault with a particular plant name (why not sage instead of salvia? Firethorn instead of pyrecantha? Something euphonious instead of a tongue-twister honouring Herr Eschscholtz? 'Many of the ancients do poorly live,' wrote Sir Thomas Browne, 'in the single names of Vegetables.') But Linnaeus's great achievement involved much more than merely putting new names to things. His classification system undertook to organize all living matter into categories and sub-categories that would not only identify them and distinguish them one from another, but would also indicate their relationships, a process that became still more important with the advent of Darwin and the theory of evolution. Therein lies one major force behind the activities of our much-maligned botanical name-changers.

According to Susyn Andrews, a taxonomist at the Royal Botanic Garden at Kew, the most upsetting cases of name changing are usually the result of reclassification, when detailed study reveals that a given plant or group of plants belongs somewhere else, or have been wrongly lumped together. For example, the genus *Sedum* is being split up into two separate genera, while *Zauschneria* is no longer regarded as a separate genus at all, but a part of *Epilobium*. So while you can still grow that pretty bush with red flowers once called *Zauschneria californica* in your rock garden (provided the climate is mild and the bed well-drained), it now answers to the name *Epilobium canum*. Other changes mentioned by Andrews include *Pratia* into *Lobelia* and *Pernettya* into *Gaultheria*. There are even vague threats to combine *Mahonia* with *Berberis*, but it hasn't happened yet, and quite possibly won't.

Lest gardeners get the idea that all these upheavals are inevitable, Susyn Andrews points out that there really are no hard and fast rules governing classification. Argument is going on constantly, and botanists (especially botanists working in different countries) are rarely in full agreement about what should be done. This lack of absolutely firm ground is clearly annoying to some precisionists, who maintain that the only way to achieve stability is to adopt strict procedures – and stick to them no matter what kind of hullabaloo ensues.

To their dismay, hullabaloo does sometimes appear to work. The garden chrysanthemum may be a case in point, though it is unlikely that anyone would admit it readily.

As is famously known, some years ago the garden chrysanthemum was moved out of the genus *Chrysanthemum* into *Dendranthema* on the basis of work done by a Russian botanist named Nikolai Tzvelev, who published his findings, buried in a huge Soviet flora, in 1961. In any genus, one particular species is designated as the type species, to which all members of the genus must be closely related; in the case of *Chrysanthemum* the type species was *C. coronarium*, the crown daisy. Until Tzvelev completed his research, *C. indicum*, the ancestor of the garden chrysanthemum, was regarded as a close relative of the crown daisy and thus a full-fledged member of the chrysanthemum tribe. Now, however, Tsevelev having decided that the two plants were really strangers, it had to leave, giving up its original genus name in favour of the relative obscurity of *Dendranthema*, and taking with it most of our autumn garden colour. (At the same time, other erstwhile chrysanthemums were also scattered, into a variety of genera ranging from *Nipponanthemum* to *Tanecetum*.)

With what has to be described as considerable reluctance, if not actual distaste, gardeners in Britain began referring to their dendranthemas instead of their chrysanthemums after *The Plant Finder* published word of the change in 1989. Elsewhere – the Netherlands, for example – the new name came into use too, though far less so in the United States. Nobody (except possibly the Dutch, who are eager to be horticulturally *au courant*) were happy about it. But so long as the crown daisy remained the touchstone of the genus *Chrysanthemum*, not much could be done about it. The only solution, a radical one, would be change the type species itself from *C. coronarium* to *C. indicum*, thereby automatically legitimizing *indicum*'s descendants, the garden cultivars. At last, in 1995, an English botanist bravely petitioned the Committee on Spermatophyta, a powerful if recherché body appointed by an international botanical congress to adjudicate such matters, to make the change. The committee voted nine to three to do so. The lowly crown daisy, mostly unmourned, was forced to depart to another genus.

This was not the first time the Committee on Spermatophyta had preserved a name – we can thank them for saving for posterity the genus names of *Petunia*, *Cytisus*, *Chaenomeles* and *Euonymus*, and a number of familiar species names including *Lycopersicon esculentum* and *Amaryllis belladonna*. Had they been available to lay down a more sensible law at the time, we might have been spared the irreparable ambiguity surrounding the word 'geranium', which is at the moment applied with greater or lesser accuracy to any one of the 550 species in the two genera of *Pelargonium* and *Geranium*.

Whether the Committee will be so accommodating in the future is a matter of debate, but in the meantime other varieties of name changes are lurking in the wings. Simple misidentification has always been a problem. A plant may be introduced and sold widely under the wrong name, as with a South African ground cover brought into Britain from Germany in 1992. It was sold as either *Bacopa* 'Snowflake' or *Sutera diffusa*. Its real name is *Sutera cordata* (*Bacopa* is a different genus and *S. diffusa* doesn't exist). Another reason for name change is when current usage violates the now-accepted rule of priority. This states that the first name given to a plant is supposed to supersede any later ones. In the past, free-wheeling botanists tended to be over-generous with names. As a letter in *The Garden* pointed out recently, an American plant we know as *Cimifuga racemosa* or black snakeroot was given no less than five different generic names and two specific epithets in the space of about a century. Shades of Farrer's campanulas!

It seems inevitable that in the matter of names there will always be a conflict of interest between botanists (who want to get it right) and gardeners (who want to get it right too, but to have it stay the same). The RHS has set up an expert Advisory Panel on Nomenclature and Taxonomy whose brief is to speak particularly for horticulturists, restricting name changes to, in the words of panel member Tony Lord, 'those that are incontrovertibly proven and helpful to gardeners'. This may be a large order, but it is certainly worth trying, and we who are still trying to remember the difference between *Gaura* and *Gaultheria* owe it a cheer.

The Ingurishu Gaaden

THE WORLDWIDE PRESTIGE of English gardening reached a sort of peak recently when a parody gardening catalogue published in the United States featured, along with the Hawes watering cans and stainless steel spades, a guaranteed authentic Imported English Gardening Couple, priced at $97,500.

While this might be regarded as nothing more than a pretty good joke – most American gardeners retain a healthy scepticism about the virtues of English-style horticulture, in spite of their susceptibility to catalogue marketing – there is one place in the world where it might just be taken seriously. Some very strange things have been going on in the land of bonsai. Japan is in the throes of a fad for English gardens and gardening.

This fact was brought home to me in a surprising way. A couple of years ago I published a collection of these pieces, most of which dealt with various aspects of English gardening, in a small book called *The Transplanted Gardener*. Not the sort of thing to appeal to Mrs Sawada in Uchinomiya, you'd think – but a Tokyo publisher actually bought the rights and published a translation in Japanese.

Though it remains to be seen whether anybody will buy my book, there's no question about the interest in the subject – apparently anything linking 'gardening' with 'England' is hot stuff in Japan these days. Bookshops and news stands are full of guidebooks to Sissinghurst and planting plans for authentic cottage gardens. Japanese tourists in England make a beeline for Hidcote or Great Dixter; I've even seen some of them wandering bemusedly through the Royal Horticultural Society's Lindley Library, as if in hope of picking up a hint or two about pleached lime walks. And speaking of the RHS, I note that the Japanese branch of that august and *echt* British organization celebrated its tenth anniversary not long ago.

To anyone who has spent time in Japan, this is an unsettling development. Japan, of course, has its own ancient and refined – perhaps over-refined – gardening tradition, based upon controlling and miniaturizing natural landscapes. It depends heavily on the use of trees, shrubs and stones, of varying foliage textures and water. Flowers play a relatively small part (unless you count cherry trees and flowering azaleas), although a certain few plants such as chrysanthemums may be grown in pots. A traditional Japanese gardener's biggest chore is probably pruning and clipping, to keep his stone pine or *Acer palmatum* looking precisely the same from year to year.

A far cry from that austere enterprise is the story told – with splendid colour photographs printed on exquisitely glossy stock – in a magazine a friend sent me from Kyoto. It's called *Plus 1 Gardening*, and this particular issue is entitled 'Small Garden' (in English and Japanese). The cover, along with several attractive pictures of flowers (roses, tulips, a hosta), shows a husky decidedly non-Japanese fellow kneeling on grass and examining what appears to be a marigold. This man, we learn from puzzling out the foreword, is Russ Yates, a professional English gardener who came to Japan in 1993. For purposes of this magazine he was hired (presumably for somewhat less than $97,500) to help a Mrs Handa Nobuko create an English-style garden surrounding her house in a Tokyo suburb.

Mrs Handa explains in her preface that she was drawn to the idea of an English garden by two things. First, she came upon a copy of the 'Yellow Book', the annual publication that lists and describes British gardens open for charity. Then she saw the movie *The Secret Garden*. Overcome by the romance of it all, she decided to go ahead. The rest of the magazine goes step by step through the process of creating the garden, including such obvious matters as drawing up a plan, preparing the ground, planting and maintenance. The closing picture shows Handa-san and Yates seated on the new wooden deck having a nice cup of (English) tea and admiring the garden.

There are a couple of significant points here. According to John Brookes, the British garden designer and writer who has worked extensively in Japan, the English garden fad is almost exclusively confined to women, mainly middle-class housewives. 'There's something very dinky-poo' about their approach, he says, including total confusion between 'design' and plain garden-making. 'They come here to England and go off to see cottage gardens in the Cotswolds, then go back and try to imitate them.' The Japanese education system, he feels, may bear some responsibility for this, because of its failure to encourage independent thinking as opposed to rote learning.

The English garden concept current in Japan is in fact 'a sort of a mirage', Brookes points out, a romantic muddle of what English gardens actually are. (There is even an American permutation of this, no less inaccurate, derived from the influence of *The Little House on the Prairie* books and television shows.) In his teaching and lectures he has tried to introduce a note of reality: 'They need to know that there is more to English gardening than a garden centre with trellises and geraniums and all sorts of English tat.' On the other hand, Brookes has sympathy for what he regards as a legitimate interest in Western-style gardening in a country that has changed as much as Japan. 'Historically, the Japanese garden tradition was never domestic, but belonged to the temple. You don't build a temple garden around a house. Now people have European houses, so they want European gardens.' That is, an *English* garden.

Why England? The American writer Pico Iyer, who lives a good part of each year in Japan, explains the current horticultural Anglophilia as part of the country's tendency to make clichés out of foreign cultures. To the average Japanese man or woman, Iyer points out, 'Germany means high philosophy, France means elegance and *couture*, American means fun. England in this scheme means everything cosy and quaint: country-houses and rolling lawns and tea-shops and teddy bears. Tweeness central.' And what could be more twee than a cottage garden, if you want to look at it that way?

Predictably enough, entrepreneurs are taking advantage of the English garden fad. For example, several years ago a businessman named Yamada Yujin imported 40,000 English bricks (the Japanese version wouldn't do) and and a team of Scottish stonemasons to build a walled garden in Nagano Prefecture. Then he hired John Brookes to design the landscaping in the best English manner and stocked the garden with nearly 3,000 plants and shrubs shipped from a nursery in Hampshire. The lawns were grown from English seed. 'When the

Japanese think of England they think of walled gardens and sweeping lawns,' Yamada was quoted as saying. Now called the Barakura English Garden, his creation covers an area of nearly two and a half acres and includes, in addition to plenty of 'sweeping lawns', a rose garden, a shop and tea room, pools, wisteria-covered pergolas and masses of flowers. It also has a philosophical position, describing itself as an 'English style garden, which is said to have lifeted [*sic*] coexistence of human being with nature up to realm of culture.' Now managed by Mrs. Kei Yamada, the garden draws up to 2,000 visitors a day in summer for a modest ¥700 (£3.80) each. A garden centre sells potted English roses next door.

Even stronger signs of the times are the rooftop English gardens blooming atop a number of big Japanese department stores. While not wholly eclipsed, miniature bonsai trees are being downgraded on grounds of cost and fiddle; the Mitsukoshi store in Tokyo recently reduced the space devoted to bonsai in favour of flowers, and in consequence tripled the sale of garden supplies and plants in a single year. John Brookes has built a garden on the roof of the Daimaru department store in Kobe, and is presently involved with creating a large (eight- or nine-acre) Western-style garden in a 'pleasure park' on the edge of Nagoya. Another will follow in Osaka. The British Department of Trade and Industry sponsored a big and successful 'English Garden' trade fair in Tokyo to show off British garden equipment (wellies, watering cans, and guaranteed English trugs are in demand), along with a mini-Chelsea of displays by nurseries and growers. (Held indoors, it went on for six weeks; Brookes, who helped to stage it, remembers how exhibitors had use relays of plants to keep their displays looking crisply English.)

Where will it all end? We probably don't need to be worried about the prospect of gnomes replacing the boulders in the great sand and stone garden of Ryoanji, though the current popularity of teddy bears is grimly suggestive. Instead – and one can only hope – in time the Handa-sans will pack up the Laura Ashley and the Earl Grey tea, and combine what they've learned about roses and campanulas and phlox with their own tradition to create something quite new under the gardening sun. It's certainly possible.

In Retrospect

The Picturesque Garden

'I like a fine prospect,' said Edward, 'but not on picturesque principles. I do not like crooked, twisted, blasted trees, I admire them much more if they are tall, straight and flourishing. I am not fond of nettles or thistles or heath blossoms.'

Marianne looked with amazement at Edward.

Sense and Sensibility by Jane Austen (1811)

A FEW MILES WEST of the old town of Ludlow in Herefordshire, the River Teme flows through a gorge choked with trees and shrubbery. The scene appears to be utterly wild, a place where the hand of man, much less gardener, cannot have disturbed the natural confusion of foliage and rippling water, distorted and shattered branches, tumbled rocks and dripping moss. Gazing into the depths, you know without seeing them that badgers and foxes must be at home here, as appropriate to the setting as the buzzard soaring silently overhead.

Hard as it may be to believe, this is a garden, an important one. Of course it has changed over the course of the two hundred years since it was first created, but not as much as you might think. In fact, if he were still on hand to lead us through his ruined grotto for a sudden view of the river, or over one of the three rustic bridges (now gone, alas), Richard Payne Knight might well feel that time and neglect had done little to damage Downton in any essential way. The wildness, the irregularity, the sense of mystery that seems to permeate the landscape would be familiar to him, and welcome.

Knight meant Downton to be revolutionary. A comfortably situated country gentleman with a taste for the arts and scholarship, he had inherited the estate – 10,000 acres, along with a good bit of money – when he was only fourteen, even before going on the obligatory grand tour to Italy. Returning from the Continent filled with enthusiasm for the villa gardens he had seen and for the paintings of artists such as Salvator Rosa and Claude Lorraine (he later formed a distinguished collection of Claude drawings), he set about designing and building a castle to live in. Typically, it was unusual. Imitation gothic on the outside, with turrets and parapets, its interiors by improbable contrast were in the grand Roman style. Even more unusual was his concept of the way the grounds around it should be landscaped.

For several decades, the reigning and all-powerful genius of British landscape design had been Lancelot 'Capability' Brown. Scarcely an estate owner with a few hundred acres to his name could be found who had not already paid Brown or one of his followers to sweep away the old terraces or knot gardens, dam up lakes and scatter clumps of trees across miles of empty lawns. ('I very earnestly wish I may die before you, Mr Brown,' an acquaintance is supposed to have said to him. 'Why so?' Brown asked. 'Because I should like to see Heaven before you had improved it.') But by the 1770s murmurings of discontent were beginning to be heard. This was the moment Knight began work on Downton, apparently determined to stay as far away from Brownian principles as he possibly could. Where Brown was smooth, he would be shaggy, intricate where Brown was grandly spacious, emotionally complex, even violent, where Brown was bland. Above all, his garden would be 'picturesque' – that is, it would duplicate, so far as possible, the effects he admired in the paintings of his favourite artists.

From descriptions by sometimes disconcerted visitors, we know a bit about what Knight achieved. For example, in 1782 a young lady named Anne Rushout noted that 'the walk afterwards brought us over a lawn where every Nettle and Thistle grows undisturbed, there were a few Rose trees just around the House but every weed had an equal share of the soil.' Others were more favourably impressed, especially by the dramatic vistas Knight had carefully opened through the trees and into the gorge, and the way he had 'enriched' the natural scenery with 'caves and cells, hovels and covered seats . . . in perfect harmony with the wild but pleasing horrors of the scene'.

We may also look to Knight himself for a notion of what he was doing at Downton. With some (though minimal) justice, he regarded himself as a writer, and had already produced books on several arcane subjects (including one called *The Worship of Priapus* on the role of the penis in pagan religion) when, in 1794, he published *The Landscape*, a long poem in heroic couplets. Its basic intent was to demolish Brown (who was by then no longer around to defend himself) and Brown's principal follower, Humphry Repton, but in passing he drops a few hints about his own approach to garden-making. These consisted very largely of, to use a famous – and frequently attacked – phrase from the poem, 'counterfeit neglect'.

What Knight seems to have meant by this was that the garden designer should aim to create scenes that matched in reality those painted landscapes by Salvator and Claude, complete with ruined buildings and broken trees and other wildly picturesque appurtenances conveying a sense of dramatic antiquity. But it had to be done subtly, by means of 'art clandestine, and conceal'd design'. The aesthetic excitement inherent in such natural phenomena as a cascade or a precipice should be preserved by the designer, though possibly enhanced by some delicate vista-cutting or pathmaking. In any event, you should never show your hand. Nature was the best judge in the end: 'Teach proud man his labour to employ/To form and decorate, and not destroy/ . . . To cherish, not mow down, the weeds that creep.'

The Landscape got a decidedly mixed reception. A writer in the *Monthly Review* went so far as to suggest that certain sections 'lead us to suspect some intervals of poetic derangement'. The poet Anna Seward detected a subversive note in Knight's over-fondness for nature, 'which must soon render our landscape-island rank, weedy, damp, and unwholesome as the uncultivate savannahs of America.' But an unstoppable tide was running in the new direction. Eccentric as Knight's opinions may have seemed to many people, they were echoed and amplified in another book published in that same year of 1794 by a second gentleman gardener, who coincidentally lived in Herefordshire only a few miles from Downton.

Uvedale Price, author of *An Essay on the Picturesque*, was the dedicatee of *The Landscape*. It is plain that he and Knight – before they both broke into print – must have spent many evenings together talking over their shared enthusiasm for landscape design and art. (They later fell out.) Where Knight was passionate but vague in verse, however, Price stuck to prose. He was also more precise about the whole subject than Knight had been, and slightly more conservative.

Price's career as a garden aesthetician had started badly. Almost his first act on inheriting his estate of Foxley a couple of decades earlier had been, 'in an unthinking moment', to demolish the old formal gardens there, with their topiary, beds and parterres. As Christopher Hussey, author of *The Picturesque*, observes, Price spent the rest of his life regretting it. As did Knight, he travelled in Italy, studied the favourite painters, and concluded that Capability's suave bareness was boring and wrong. In his mature view, 'all types of gardens must be judged by universal principles of painting'. But this did not entail trying to copy paintings, or falling back on 'unembellished nature'. It was much more a matter of understanding and deploying the essentials of the painter's art – colour, light and shade. Massing forms, manipulating dense and transparent, making discreet use of contrasts in colour or shape: these were what garden designers should bear in mind, whatever the scale they worked on.

Especially in later essays, Price got more specific, discussing such subjects as 'artificial water' and the way its edges could be adorned with shrubs, and 'decorations near the house'. Unlike Knight, he did not argue for barely cooked nature; he could see the virtues in avenues, and even suggested the planting of climbing vines against walls and over rocks. Given that at the end of the eighteenth century landscape design had been almost totally divorced from horticulture, he had little to say for or about flowers (except in drifts along banks, growing naturally) but his implication that handsomely planted terraces and formal gardens close to the house were not only acceptable but desirable opened the way to their return from exile. Luckily too – because this was exactly the time when the wholesale introduction of new species from distant corners of the globe was about to begin in earnest.

At the end of the eighteenth century, however, picturesque was the word of the day. A Yorkshire clergyman named William Gilpin had for years been making an extremely good thing of it, travelling around the country locating and describing authentic picturesque scenes and writing influential books about them; he eventually published no less than eight richly illustrated volumes. (Among Gilpin's dicta: the most picturesque animal is a cow, and 'cows are commonly the most picturesque in the months of April and May, when the old hair is coming off.' Dying or blasted trees are 'the very capital sources of picturesque beauty'.) Writers like Jane Austen and Thomas Love Peacock joked about it, while architects reached for picturesque irregularity in their plans. The Age of Reason was giving way to the Age of Romance.

Poor Repton, as the standard-bearer of the old school of landscape design, hardly stood a chance. Disdained by Gilpin and attacked by both Knight and Price for too slavishly following Capability Brown, he attempted to defend himself, spluttering that 'propriety and convenience are not less objects of good taste than picturesque effect'. More significantly, however, he gradually altered his own practice, and before long was introducing elements of the picturesque in his design schemes. If this did not include Knight's 'weeds that creep', it did involve terraces and formal gardens, and plantings that at least hinted at what William Robinson and Gertrude Jekyll would achieve – with a vastly expanded repertoire of flowers and shrubs – seventy-five years later.

Knight himself seems to have moderated some of his more extreme ideas as time passed. He granted that the house itself needed a comfortable setting, and argued for Italian-style 'terraces and borders intermixed with vines and flowers' – a far cry from blasted trees. He gradually tired of life as a bachelor in a castle, and in 1809 moved to his house in London, retaining only a cottage at Downton. The estate became the property of his brother Thomas, a distinguished pomologist and later president of the Horticultural Society. It is possible that Thomas preferred apples and pears to landscape gardening. In any case, the first picturesque garden gradually, inexorably, returned to its wild state, not having very far to go. Today, appropriately, it is a nature reserve.

The Fever Bark Tree

Treatment [of malaria]. This is comprised in one word: Quinine.
Sir William Osler, 1917

O F ALL THE MEDICINES DERIVED from plants, quinine may be the best known. It has been in use by Europeans for nearly 400 years and probably a lot longer than that by native peoples. An alkaloid derived from the bark of an attractive shiny-leafed evergreen tree called cinchona, it has a remarkable ability to control and cure the highly dangerous, often deadly, intermittent fever of malaria.

Throughout history, however, there's been a big problem with quinine: the trees it comes from grow in one of the world's most inaccessible, inhospitable spots – the sodden, jungle-choked gorges and valleys on the eastern flank of the Andes. Until the middle of the nineteenth century, in fact, they grew nowhere else. The world was dependent for its supply of the life-saving bark on the activities of Peruvian and Bolivian collectors known as *cascarilleros*, who searched out the trees and stripped them, generally killing them in the process.

In addition to its geographic obscurity, there had always been a certain amount of confusion and controversy about 'the fever bark tree'. Even its genus name *Cinchona*, given it by the botanist Linnaeus, incorporated a mispelling (it should have been *Chinchona*, after a seventeenth-century Duchess of Chinchón, who was Spanish; Linnaeus apparently confused the pronunciation with Italian). First introduced into Europe by Jesuit priests, for a long time the bark was viewed with deep suspicion in Protestant countries, and acceptance was slow in spite of its use in curing such distinguished patients as the Queen of Spain and a son of Louis XIV. But by 1820 chemists had managed to isolate the principal active element, and soon quinine sulphate was being produced commercially from the bark. Yet the only source remained the cinchona tree, lost in its remote forests.

The obvious solution was to grow cinchona trees where they were easier to reach for harvesting. That meant transplanting, or at least securing viable seeds, but attempts to accomplish this had been markedly unsuccessful if not disastrous. In 1743 the French astronomer Charles de la Condamine nursed a collection of young plants for eight months during a 2,500-mile journey down the Amazon, only to have them washed overboard as he reached the Atlantic. His botanist colleague, Joseph de Jussieu, spent fifteen laborious years studying cinchona and other plants in the South American forests (he was the first to examine and send to Europe specimens of coca, the source of cocaine), but at the end of his travails all of his collections were stolen, whereupon Jussieu went mad.

Had poor Jussieu managed to retain his collections and his sanity, the path to a dependable supply of quinine might have been more direct. European ignorance about the botany of cinchona was profound. Few realized that there was not just one kind of tree but dozens, with subspecies ranging from shrubby dwarfs to eighty-foot forest giants, and that they grew over a broad range from Bolivia to Venezuela. Moreover, their barks varied widely in quinine content, so much so that some shipments reaching London or Amsterdam were virtually worthless. As a result, cinchona got such a bad name that in certain medical circles doctors refused to prescribe it.

The first serious attempt to transplant cinchona trees foundered on this ignorance, but not before a great deal of effort and expense had been devoted to it. In 1852 a botanist named J. C. Hasskarl sailed off to South America under orders from the Dutch government to collect plants and transport them to the malaria-ridden Netherlands East Indies. After many adventures he succeeded in smuggling four or five hundred seedlings of a variety thought to be rich in quinine out of Bolivia, along with many seeds, including some helpfully supplied by the Dutch consul in La Paz. When he finally reached Java (aboard a Dutch warship commandeered for the journey) most of the seedlings were dead, but the undaunted Hasskarl went ahead to propagate the seeds and establish plantations of the most vigorous varieties. It wasn't until years later, when the trees were big enough to harvest, that it became apparent that he had chosen a species of cinchona containing practically no quinine at all.

Now it was the turn of the British. Clements Markham, later Sir Clements, KCB, FRS, was no botanist, but a public-minded explorer, geographer and man of letters of the sort that only Victorian England produced. He conceived the notion that bringing a cheap and convenient supply of quinine to the malarial masses of India would be a laudable enterprise. Granted government funding in 1859, he organized several teams of explorers and gardeners to collect cinchona plants of different types in various regions. He would himself head for the central Andes to collect the most promising species: *Cinchona calisaya*. Markham also made a public announcement of what he intended to do, which – given the economic dependence of countries like Bolivia on their cinchona bark exports – was probably not a very smart move. That locals might not share his wish to do good on a large scale never seems to have occurred to him, although he was right in stressing that their continued ravaging of the cinchona forests would inevitably lead to extinction.

In his 1880 book *Peruvian Bark*, Markham describes the achievements of the search parties, naturally concentrating on his own harrowing experiences. Skirting the Bolivian border on the far side of Lake Titicaca, he soon ran into opposition in the form of a red-faced heavy named Martel who declared that anybody attempting to take cinchona out of the country would be seized and his feet cut off. Markham naturally ignored the threats and proceeded down into the gorges in search of *C. calisaya*, which he eventually found, but not before dealing with 'venemous [*sic*] insects', jaguars, huge snakes, hornets, bears, a plague of butterflies, and 'giddy precipices'. The Indian guides became mutinous when they ran out of coca leaves to chew (Markham had his own supply), and the whole crew nearly starved. But they emerged from the rainforest with some 500 *calisaya* seedlings bundled in matting, and by taking a roundabout route in order to evade Martel and his cohorts, made it back to the coast safely.

It would be nice to report that Markham's efforts paid off, but every one of his plants died *en route* to India. Another of his teams, led by Richard Spruce, an intrepid botanist-explorer, had better luck – of a sort. They travelled into Ecuador to collect *C. succirubra*, 'red bark' cinchona, which in Markham's (mistaken) opinion was a first-rate source of quinine. *Cascarilleros* had already killed off most of the trees, but they managed to amass more than 600 seedlings and thousands of seeds, which reached India in good condition. The same could not be said for Spruce, who suffered a paralytic attack while deep in the forest, and though he bravely kept working was left an invalid for the remaining thirty-three years of his life.

Markham's account has a faintly triumphant tone. Huge cinchona plantations – in Ceylon, in Sikkim, in a number of locations in India proper – had been established by the time he wrote it, mainly stocked with red bark trees. But it was even then clear, in spite of Markham's optimism, that *C. succirubra* was simply not good enough as a quinine source. Another irony was in the making.

Living in the village of Puno on Lake Titicaca, at the very time Markham had passed through (though the two apparently never met) was an Englishman named Charles Ledger, who made his living as a broker dealing in bark and alpaca wool. Ledger was no stick-in-the-mud – he once attempted to introduce alpacas to Australia, shepherding a flock the whole way himself, but they died – and as a dealer knew a good bit about cinchona. He also possessed an exceptional contact in Manuel Incra Mamani, a Bolivian *cascarillero* who had previously worked for years as Ledger's servant. In 1865 Mamani turned up in Puno after a remarkable mid-winter trek across the mountains to offer Ledger a package of cinchona seeds, reportedly from the best tree in a remote grove of the best true calisayas. Ledger paid him £150 and sent him back for more, in the meantime carefully drying the seeds and sending them to his brother George in London to be sold. (On the second trip Mamani was caught, jailed, starved and beaten; he refused to tell what he had done with the seeds, and died soon after being released.)

In London, however, nobody wanted the seeds. Too much government money had already been sunk into Markham's enterprise. George Ledger finally managed to unload half of them to a planter who took them to India (where they vanished from history). The other half went for a modest price to the Dutch government, which in spite of the

Hasskarl fiasco still harbored hopes of growing cinchona in Java and was apparently willing to take a flyer.

Cinchona ledgeriana, as it came to be called, turned out to be the answer. The seeds germinated and grew well in Java, the trees proved to be rich in quinine, and before long the Dutch were in happy possession of a monopoly. The Indian plantations could not compete. In 1876 a private grower was the first to root up his red bark trees, and within a decade nearly all of the plantings had been converted to tea or allowed to return to wilderness. Her Majesty's Treasury took the brunt of the cost, while until the beginning of World War II the Dutch East Indies remained the primary source for cinchona and quinine.

The ironies that mark the cinchona story were not quite over yet. War stimulated the development of improved anti-malarials, notably the drug chloroquine, and quinine seemed superseded for good. Even the *ledgeriana* plantations of Java were no longer worth the upkeep. The delicate trees had never been easy to cultivate, normally needing to be raised under special conditions of temperature and shade, and then grafted onto more vigorous stock. Moreover, stripping the bark usually killed them. It made simple economic sense to forget about them and move on to some more promising crop.

Consequently, there was almost no new quinine being produced anywhere when, thirty years ago, medical scientists first realized that chloroquine had stopped working against certain strains of malaria bacteria, and that the resistant strains were spreading rapidly in all malaria-prone regions of the world. Quinine still worked, and still does. It has been synthesized, but the best source is still cinchona. So derelict plantations are being cleaned up and new ones planted. The long career of the fever-bark tree still has some way to go.

Appleseed's Seedlings

THE WELSH MARCHES, especially Herefordshire over into Monmouthshire, is old apple country. In the past every cottage had a few distinctly local trees, varieties with names now obscure or forgotten. There was a small orchard at Towerhill Cottage when we arrived, and we have kept it going, replanting when decay and a December gale took out several of the older top-heavy standards. The only survivor I've able to name for sure is an 'Egremont Russet'. It somehow seems important to maintain the orchard tradition, although it's hard to know what to do with all the apples. The fact is, you get fond of apple trees.

Something of this same affection must have been carried to America with the first emigrants, and by their descendants across the continent. An apple tree is a wonderfully generous thing, productive of some sort of fruit (however misshapen or wormy) no matter what little care it gets once it is big enough to resist a grazing deer or cow. That alone must have made it precious to a settler struggling to raise a crop of barley or corn amid the stumps of a poorly-cleared woodland.

No wonder he loved to tell tales about that authentic American oddball John Chapman, otherwise known as Johnny Appleseed, who made it his life's occupation to scatter apple trees all through the Old Northwest Territory – Ohio, Indiana, Michigan, Illinois – when it was still the frontier, between about 1800 and 1840.

Just how good, though, were Appleseed's apples? The story goes that he made a practice of collecting the seed of good apples from families who put him up for the night. He would then plant the seed in patches in the wilderness, where they would sprout and be ready to fill pies when the first hungry pioneers moved into the region. It is a pleasant story, and not altogether inaccurate.

Johnny indeed grew trees from seed, as did almost everyone else importing apples from more settled country, beginning with the first immigrants from the Old World, because seed is a great deal more portable than saplings. (You can get 300,000 apple seeds into a bushel basket.) But instead of accumulating apple cores, he usually followed the traditional custom of collecting his seeds from the pomace left over from cider-making at mills further east. Moreover, he took care to make proper plantations and fence them against wild animals. (I'm not sure what he did about mice and chipmunks, which can – and do – consume apple seed eagerly before it has a chance to sprout.) Sometimes he would stay around long enough to tend the trees until they were big enough to transplant; sometimes he would simply leave them, fenced, knowing that settlers would find them when they arrived. On many occasions he sold the little trees to farmers to support more gathering and planting. His nurseries were often substantial – one at Milan on the Huron River in Michigan (only a few miles from my home town, by the way, which was founded in 1820) had 15,000 trees in it.

Apples raised from seed, however, are notoriously undependable so far as quality is concerned. In his classic compendium *The Apples of New York*, published in 1905, S. A. Beach remarked that cultivated varieties 'seldom, if ever, reproduce true from seed', and that 'it is not to be wondered that our common apples are mongrels'. Anyone who has ever lived in the vicinity of a former cider mill, as I once did in the Berkshires, and tasted the apples on the wild trees growing scattered around the site will know what this means. The problem is that (except for a few relatively unusual strains) a seed will almost inevitably have been cross-fertilized, and apples on a tree raised from it will share genes from both its parents. More often than not, the result is a bad apple. In the old days, in fact, such nameless types were known as 'common' apples and used for cider or animal feed.

This need not always be the case. Even a mongrel can be beautiful. It has been estimated that one out of ten seed-raised apples is acceptable, and perhaps one out of a hundred actually good. Before the days of deliberate cross-breeding and gene manipulation, such random mating gave birth to every new variety, including the most prized. Quite apart from possible improved quality, it was the only way apples suited to new climatic and soil conditions could be developed. Thus very few of the famous English varieties – 'Cox's Orange Pippin', 'Worcester Pearmain', 'Blenheim Orange' etc. – ever made much headway in the United States, where native variations like 'Northern Spy', 'Esopus Spitzenburg' and more recently 'Jonathan' took over. A hundred years ago, Beach noted how in the region beyond the Great Lakes 'the varieties succeeding best are selections from seedlings which have originated in that region.'

Yet even if the odds could be improved, raising apples from seed requires patience. You probably won't see fruit for up to seven years, and that's if you are lucky. If at that point you learn you have a good new selection amid your forest of dim and uninteresting specimens, there is only one way to reproduce it – by grafting. Only a grafted apple will come true.

Johnny Appleseed, among his numerous quirks and strong opinions, was absolutely opposed to pruning and grafting. This seems to have been part of his Swedenborgian religious convictions, which also included vegetarianism, refusal to ride a horse or wear fur, and a belief, as one writer put it, that apple trees in their flowering were a living sermon from God. His one dependable biographer, Robert Price, describes him as a man with 'the thick bark of queerness' on him. All of which must have done a great deal to encourage his legend, without necessarily improving the quality of his apples.

Writing in 1867, an Ohio doctor and pomologist by avocation named John Warder remarks that Appleseed ('a singular being, more savage than polished') was 'useful in his way', but it was 'to the intelligent nurseryman that we are especially indebted' for the spread of good apples across 'our extended country'. He goes on to point out the way certain apple varieties moved from east to west along with settlers from different regions. Western New York, for example, received its early fruit from Connecticut and Massachusetts, and then in turn passed it on, duly modified, to Michigan, northern Illinois and, later, Wisconsin and Iowa. Ohio and Indiana got theirs mainly from New Jersey and Pennsylvania, Kentucky from Virginia, Tennessee from Virginia and North Carolina. All these last then thrust further west into southern Indiana, southern Illinois, Mississippi and Arkansas, where –

at least in the 1860s when Warder was writing – you could identify the source of emigrants from the kind of apple trees they were growing.

None of this would have possible, of course, without grafting, which was not practised widely in the United States until after 1800. No choice variety could survive longer than the life of the original tree. And raising seedlings and grafting them was the business of the 'intelligent nurseryman'. There were plenty of these. One splendid example, who certainly deserves to share a little of Johnny Appleseed's fame, was Henderson Lewelling, who established a flourishing fruit nursery in Henry County, Iowa, in the late 1830s. Local success wasn't enough for Lewelling, however, and in 1847 he set out for the Oregon Territory in a wagon train that included a specially-designed travelling nursery filled with 700 plants ranging from grafted apple whips to grapevines. Seven months later, after a harrowing trip during which half of his greenery died, he reached the Willamette Valley and began planting. Some of the surviving young trees had grown as much as three feet *en route*. Within a few years he was supplying settlers with apple and other fruit trees – including the sweet, dark bing cherry, a lucky discovery grown from an anonymous cherry pit he happened to have brought along from Iowa, and named after a Chinese workman.

Lewelling later went on to California, and eventually even to Honduras, a nurseryman all the way. Johnny Appleseed, on the other hand, came to a halt in northern Indiana, where he died in 1845, leaving a prodigious number of half-wild apple trees, biblical tracts, and campfire tales behind him. A few years ago, word came that the last one of the old man's trees was still alive, though barely, on a farm near the village of Nova, Ohio. It was described as being his favourite variety, 'Rambo', 'firm and tart,' and suitable for either cooking or eating. Horticulturists from an organization called American Forests quickly stepped in and took cuttings from the tree (which was lucky because a storm toppled it three years later). Grafted with buds, the resulting saplings will go on sale soon. While it probably isn't worth speculating on just how Appleseed managed to propagate his favourite from seed in the first place without some impious grafting, I don't doubt for a moment that the new lot will be first-rate. I wouldn't mind having one to fill in next to the 'Egremont Russet' at Towerhill Cottage.

The Bishop's Garden

O NE OF THE LEAST ATTRACTIVE expressions in the whole realm of gardening must be 'plant material'. Landscape architects use it all the time. Of course they are in the business of creating effects, not breeding pansies or coaxing a wisteria to bloom, so perhaps they can be excused. But talk of 'plant material' has always struck me as a bit insulting to the plants themselves. How would you like to be referred to as 'human material'?

I'm firmly on the side of the plantsman or woman, the person who evinces real affection for each of his or her charges, is curious about its likes and dislikes, treasures it in spite of its failings, and never thinks of it as 'material'. I'm glad to say that there are still plenty of gardeners like that around today, and probably always will be. But the true springtime of the plantsman, I am convinced, was some 400 years ago, in the heart of the Renaissance. I'm led to this conclusion by a book I came across recently, a book about a book about a garden.

Hortus Eystettensis ('The Garden of Eichstätt'), first published in 1613, has been described as the greatest botanical picture book ever created. Certainly it was one of the biggest. An enormous thing containing some 367 plates depicting more than a thousand different plants, it was bound in two volumes so large that according to one commentator they had to be moved in a wheelbarrow. Sir Thomas Browne called the book the 'massiest' of herbals. It was also without question one of the loveliest, especially the hand-coloured copies. These cost a staggering 500 florins, at a time when a head gardener could be hired for 60 florins a year.

Thanks to an exceptional piece of modern bookmaking, we can get a sense of this beauty at a somewhat more reasonable price. Under the auspices of the British Library, the bibliographical scholar Nicholas Barker has published, in large folio size, a study of the book with many pages in reproduction and a fascinating text. Browsing through it, I couldn't help being struck not only by the technical excellence of the plant illustrations, but also by the evident freshness, sometimes even amounting to surprise, with which the artists viewed the plants themselves. It was as if these unique living objects were being examined carefully for the first time. In some cases, of course – newly bred tulip crosses, for example, or the enormous *Agave americana* – they really were.

The original publisher of *Hortus Eystettensis* was a botanist-apothecary of Nuremberg named Basileus Besler. It was Besler who oversaw the teams of painters, engravers and colourists, and it was Besler who found the buyers, mostly minor princes and rich burghers building libraries and collecting plants of their own. Behind the book, however, was a garden, and a gardener, by all odds a most unusual gardener.

Johann Conrad von Gemmingen became Bishop of Eichstätt, a small diocese halfway between Munich and Nuremberg, in 1595, when he was thirty-four. He was already rich, and was to get richer through family inheritances. He was well-educated, and had travelled in Italy, France and England, cultivating, in the words of one acquaintance, 'a policy of few words, open ears and an open mind, journeying not as spiders but as bees'. There is an unconfirmed story that as a young man in England he served as a page to Elizabeth I.

The Bishop's palace perched atop a steep hill called the Willibaldburg overlooking the River Altmuhl and the town of Eichstätt. Not the easiest place to build a garden, perhaps, but that hardly deterred Johann Conrad. Amidst his many official duties – he was apparently tough on witches, but liberal in his relations with Jews, relaxing various prohibitions – he set about designing a complicated and expensive new layout for the palace and its grounds. The basic aim was to create spaces and suitable environments to grow a vast variety of plants – not only vegetables, fruit and medicinal herbs, but also plants distinguished purely by their beauty or rarity. This was something new.

The second half of the sixteenth century was an exciting and expansive time in plantsmanship. 'Never before or since,' says historian

William Stearn, 'has there been such an astonishing influx of colourful strange plants,' largely from Turkey and the Near East – lilies, tulips, irises, anemones and crown fritillaries. More were coming from the Americas. And with this abundance there was increasing interest in growing flowers and developing new cultivars. In his *De Historia Stirpium* (1542) Leonhard Fuchs listed only about 500 plants; by 1623 Caspar Bauhin could describe more than 6000. For a sophisticated nobleman like the Bishop of Eichstätt, moved not only by an interest in science and the collection of rarities, but also by a theological impulse to understand and celebrate God's grace in creating the natural world, botany was a logical predilection.

Four hundred years on, in the wake of countless wars and many generations of plant life, we would be unlikely to have any first-hand impression of the bishop's garden except for a lucky accident. In March 1611, a much-traveled art dealer from Augsburg named Philipp Hainhofer came on a semi-diplomatic visit. He was a sort of royal go-between, an agent acting as a scout, a collector, and information-gatherer, and his call on the Bishop of Eichstätt involved making enquiries on behalf of one of his princely patrons. Fortuitously, Hainhofer's visit came at a time when the Bishop's garden-making was in full swing, and work on the great florilegium had already begun.

As the Bishop himself was indisposed when Hainhofer arrived (he was actually very ill 'from a congestion in the lungs', and would die the next year), his steward and chamberlain escorted the visitor around the episcopal palace. There were, according to Hainhofer's account, eight different gardens, each containing plants from a different country, varying in the style of the beds and the flowers, 'especially the beautiful roses, lilies, tulips, among other flowers.' The gardens were partly adorned with painted walls and pleasure rooms, and apparently linked by pavilions. Each garden had its own gardener in charge, and 'none infringes on the other's domain'.

The next day Hainhofer passed through glassed galleries outside the Bishop's rooms filled with plants – pansies (red, yellow, brown, and speckled) in flowerpots, and tubs of violets, apricots, pomegranates, lemons and the enamel-leafed *Amaranthus tricolor*. These could apparently be moved outdoors during the summer and then into the heated galleries for the cold weather. Outside, on the balconies, six large blocks of wood served as bases to support as many dead trees where in the winter singing birds would come and be fed to entertain the Bishop. Other fragments of information suggest that he had accumulated many extremely costly varieties of plants, including, by his own boast, 'tulips in five hundred colours, almost all different'.

Where did the plants for what the Bishop improbably called his 'modest, narrow little garden' come from? In a letter to Hainhofer's patron, he explained that he had secured them 'through the offices of local merchants' from the Netherlands, 'for example from Antwerp, Brussels, Amsterdam and other places'. These were, of course, the principal transhipment points for rare plants from all over the world at the time, especially from Turkey and the Near East (narcissi, hyacinths, tulips of course), but also such plants as sunflowers, nicotianas, evening primroses, Michaelmas daisies and so on from the New World. And with the unprecedented new taste for flowers, even native German weeds were being crossbred or introduced in their original forms for garden use.

It is clear from his comprehensive interest in collecting and growing unusual plants that the Bishop of Eichstätt was a true plantsman, but we have far stronger proof. It lies in the grand book named after his garden and illustrating its contents (and other plants), the *Hortus Eystettensis*. Hainhofer notes that at the time of his visit the Bishop's 'most precious drawings' – the plant pictures he had been commissioning from a range of artists – were not in the palace but had been sent to Basileus Besler in Nuremberg, to be used in the preparation of a book which he intended to publish. In addition, 'one or two boxes full of fresh flowers' were being dispatched to Besler each week to be sketched.

Unfortunately the Bishop did not live to see his book completed. Besler took over, financing the project and eventually publishing the huge volumes successfully; reprints, from the original plates, continued to appear for more than 200 years. *Hortus Eystettensis* remains a landmark not only in botany but in art, an extraordinary expression of the painter and engraver's skill but even more of the beauty of the plants themselves, a testament to the plantsman's ethic. The coloured copies – Barker estimates that between twenty and thirty survive – are treasured and literally priceless rarities.

Judging from Hainhofer's description of the amount of building work still going on only shortly before the Bishop's death, we may assume that the garden, like the book, was far from finished. (What garden ever is?) The new Bishop kept it up to a degree, though not on quite the same plan; in the 1630s, along with much of Central Europe, the palace on the mountain was ravaged in the Thirty Years War. In the early eighteenth century another bishop 'improved' the garden, laying out paths, shrubs and trees. After that, it fell into disuse, to the point where there was scarcely a garden to be seen. At the start of the nineteenth century, a local official lamented that it was now impossible to make out its location. Explorations of the ruins atop the Willibaldsburg revealed just four living reminders of the fact that a great plantsman had once gardened here: a snapdragon, a garden violet, honeysuckle and a yellow horned poppy.

The Quaker Axis

HORTICULTURE OWES A LOT to the Quakers. Perhaps it was chance, perhaps it was something in their peaceable faith that drew them toward science and the natural world, but one thing is clear: without the devotion and enthusiasm of two Quakers in particular – John Bartram in Philadelphia and Peter Collinson in London – the great eighteenth-century movement of American plants into the gardens of Europe could hardly have happened.

In America today, Bartram is certainly the better known of the two. He was the explorer, the adventurer and plant-hunter, a barely educated farmer who turned himself by sheer willpower into a botanist of skill and great practical experience. Born near Philadelphia in 1699, he built a house beside the Schuylkill River and created a notable garden. (It is now restored and protected as a park, a pocket of greenery in the depths of a fairly grim industrial suburb.)

Plants had interested Bartram profoundly from youth. Teaching himself enough Latin to read botanical texts, he began identifying and collecting native species. When he could afford to leave the farm for a few weeks at a time (usually in autumn after the harvest, when wild plants had set seed), he would go off on collecting trips into the still-unexplored interior. Money, however, was short, the more so when his expeditions began getting in the way of his husbandry.

Philadelphia, fortunately, was no backwater. Bartram's own cousin, Humphrey Marshall, was a distinguished botanist there; sophisticated men like Benjamin Franklin and other leading figures (most of them Quakers) were among Bartram's acquaintances. Word of his skills as a plant-collector must have already been widespread when the London merchant Peter Collinson put it about that he was looking for someone able to supply him with New World specimens. In about 1733 the two men began corresponding.

Peter Collinson had made his fortune in the family business as a draper and haberdasher ('They are as much busied in how to increase their wealth and riches as any,' a contemporary commentator dourly remarked of the otherwise sober Quakers), and developed a love of plants as a boy in his grandmother's suburban garden. Natural history was an obsession. His own first garden attracted the admiration of the Swedish botanist Peter Kalm, who described it as 'beautiful . . . full of all kinds of the rarest plants, especially American'; a year or two after Kalm's visit Collinson moved to Mill Hill on the northern edge of London and began work on a botanical garden that would eventually become one of the most famous of its time.

Collinson did his best to secure rare plants wherever he could. 'Oh for the peep of a new thing,' he once wrote, 'how it revives the flagging spirit.' French missionaries in China sent him an ailanthus and some camellias; the Tzar's English physician sent him hornbeam seeds from Persia. But, as Kalm had noticed, Collinson was particularly keen on American plants. Not only were there huge numbers of new species being found, but many had the appeal of hardiness in England. This was particularly true of plants from the Middle Atlantic States.

By the time Collinson got in touch with Bartram, he was beginning to despair of finding a dependable source of American species. Odds and ends had come through – seeds of saxifrage and dittany from Maryland, raspberries from New England. He had contributed funding to the explorations of the English naturalist Mark Catesby in the Carolinas and Georgia (and may have received some specimens or seeds from him, though most of Catesby's hard-won collections were destroyed by pirates *en route* back to England). Catesby's reports made Collinson more than ever aware, as he wrote to a friend, that 'what were common with them would very likely be rare in England'. Yet his many attempts to get American correspondents to send plants all failed. 'It is needless to tell thee with what industry I have cultivated friendship and acquaintance with the principal men of North America,' he complained. 'Great promises but slender performances.'

In Bartram, Collinson found exactly what he was looking for and, as their correspondence shows, he took pains with the relationship. It would not have done to get Bartram's back up. Given the economic difference between them (to say nothing of various other gaps), the situation called for tact. Collinson's solution was pretend that the arrangement called simply for mutually beneficial trades on a relaxed basis. 'I only bear mention these plants,' he would write, 'not that I expect thee to send them. I don't expect or desire them, but as they happen to be found accidentally . . .' He also made a point of sending seeds back to Bartram, including nuts and vines and on one occasion a selection of sixty-nine 'curious' varieties chosen by Philip Miller of the Chelsea Physic Garden.

Gradually, however, the eastward flow of plants predominated, and to some extent took over Collinson. 'I am like the parson's barn, I refuse nothing,' he advised Bartram, supplying him with paper for drying specimens and telling him how to build containers for the transport of live plants like laurels and honeysuckles. He also worried about him. When war in the 1750s made travel dangerous even in hitherto peaceful Pennsylvania, Collinson wrote to say that he hoped his 'old friend' would not 'expose himself to Indian cruelties. And yet,' he went on, 'I want a dozen boxes of seeds.'

With Bartram doing most of the work, the idea of a plain gentlemen's exchange agreement had to go by the boards. At first Collinson came through with token 'gifts' – a suit of clothes, books, a magnifying glass and a compass, cloth for another suit. Sometimes he misjudged his gifts, as when he sent a velvet cap, evidently a cast-off, and Bartram complained that it was full of holes. Collinson also slipped occasionally into a tone of paternal condescension, for example telling Bartram how he should dress when visiting some Virginian magnate, and criticizing his prose style. But he seems to have done his best to stay on the right side of his correspondent, providing introductions, offering botanical information, and displaying honest warmth and friendship in his letters. In time money too came into the picture.

Bartram had suggested that the proprietors of the Pennsylvania colony might be willing to pay him an annual salary in exchange for his botanical services. This idea came to nothing (though he did get permission to use the Philadelphia Library free for life) but Collinson had a better plan. News of his new supplier of rarities had spread quickly in England, where there was no shortage of wealthy or well-placed connoisseurs eager to share in the largesse. Miller at the Chelsea Physic Garden was one; others included the Duke of Richmond, Lord Petre, Dr John Fothergill (another Quaker), and Sir Hans Sloane, president of the Royal Society. Soon Bartram found himself packing up seeds to be sent to a wide variety of eager English collectors. Collinson, Miller and the Duke of Richmond initially agreed to fund Bartram's plant-hunting expeditions themselves; eventually Collinson raised a subscription giving him twenty guineas a year for travelling expenses.

Before long Bartram was devoting several months a year to collecting. Collinson served as his unpaid middleman (not always with great efficiency; the Londoner had a tendency to muddle the accounts and throw away letters), passing on requests and distributing seeds and plants. In later years, Bartram's 'five-guinea box' containing a selection of seeds of 105 trees and shrubs, each carefully labelled, became famous. His practice was to collect plants and seeds in the wild, then raise them in his own garden, thus securing large supplies ready for shipment.

The Quaker axis continued to function for more than thirty years, until revolution broke out in 1776. Collinson died in 1768; Bartram nine years later, to be succeeded by his son William as an explorer (if less assiduous plant supplier). Through Collinson's efforts, John Bartram received a royal appointment as the King's Botanist in the North American colonies (with £50 a year); for his part Collinson, thanks largely to Bartram, could claim to have introduced or cultivated for the first time in England at least 171 species of plants, including half a dozen different lilies, beebalm, *Potentilla fruticosa*, poison oak, *Trillium undulatum* (which a thief stole from Collinson's garden), the Turkey oak and the witch alder (*Fothergilla major*).

Though he was sometimes at a loss as to how to grow his 'exoticks' – regarding *Xerophyllum asphodeloides*, Collinson was reduced to pleading with Bartram to 'give me a hint how to manage this intractable vegetable' – the Quaker merchant never ceased to yearn for still more treasures from America. 'I have a sprig (in flower) of the *Kalmia* [*latifolia*],' he wrote in 1761, 'and it stares me in the face all the while I am writing, saying or seeming to say, 'As you are so fond of me, tell my friend, John Bartram, who sent me, to send more to keep me company; for they will be sure to be well nursed and well treated.'

Birds in the Garden

B IRDS IN THE GARDEN are generally regarded as a Good Thing. It would take far more than the space I have here to enumerate their virtues, even if I confined myself to their songs. Nothing could be more chillingly provocative than Rachel Carson's classic title; a 'silent spring' is about as abhorrent a prospect as one could conceive, and the very thought of no more blackbirds in England – or catbirds in New England – induces gloom. This is not to say that every sound emitted by a bird is pleasant. For the last month or so we have been putting up with a cock pheasant who sleeps high in a larch tree ten yards from Towerhill Cottage. The problem is that he seems to think he is a rooster. Every morning at precisely 6:30 he announces dawn with fifteen minutes of short sleep-shattering squawks delivered with metronomic precision, like a gargantuan leaky tap. Then he flies off, squawking.

He is not the first bird I've had trouble with. I still recall with pain blundering through a pitch-dark campground in Connecticut trying to silence an invisible but tireless whippoorwill with chunks of firewood. (A whippoorwill is a particularly noisy American form of nightjar.) A berserk woodpecker in the Massachusetts Berkshires, having driven himself mad by mistaking a telephone switchbox for a hollow tree, once very nearly drove me mad too. Yet I'm not among those for whom a wood full of nesting rooks, swooping and hollering, possesses all the charm of a six-lane motorway running past the front door. With birds you have to take the rough with the smooth.

The 'smooth', for most gardeners, is the happy willingness of many common birds to eat insects, weed seeds and other small unwanted objects that we can't deal with on our own without recourse to lethal chemicals. While I am not an organic gardener on principle, I find that I need to use almost no insecticides on the veg or to spray the fruit trees because our large resident bird population appears willing to do the job for me. Of course there are occasional confusions – the famous failure of some finches to discriminate between fruit buds and bud-shaped insects while dining may be laid either to ignorance or malice, depending on how you feel about finches. The fact remains that the gardener gets no fruit. And Christopher Lloyd is prepared to blame English birds for damaging the buds on everything from Japanese quinces to wisteria. Possibly our birds are better behaved, or less stupid, than his, but so far they've left the buds alone, sensibly preferring ripe cherries and raspberries.

Over the course of centuries small birds have had a rougher time of it than gardeners. When they weren't being shot for food (the propensity of French and Italian hunters to blast away at anything on wings, even today, was shared by sportsmen in England and America until well into the nineteenth century), they were being poisoned, netted, sold as cage birds, stuffed for collectors and otherwise dispatched. Farmers and gardeners alike had little sympathy for them, believing that unless they (along with rats, mice and other vermin) were controlled, crops losses would be insupportable. The slaughter was sometimes spectacular. In 1779, for example, 4,152 birds were killed in one Lincolnshire village alone. Fourteen thousand perished in a nearby parish during a ten-year period. In the United States, boys customarily went out shooting all sorts of small songbirds on Election Day until the 1860s, and American robins – plucked for roasting – continued to bring a good price in city markets for quite a bit longer. (The American robin is actually a red-breasted thrush, and larger than the English version. Not much larger, though.)

Apart from enjoying their company (sometimes), most gardeners *like* birds but have never been completely easy with them. Gratitude for their good works has always been tempered with suspicion, plus a certain failure to accept reality. Possibly the best single illustration of how wrong things can go between birds and people was an episode in nineteenth-century America known as the Great Sparrow War, a sequence of events that began with misplaced affection and ended with mass murder – and a new bird fluttering through gardens from Maine to California.

The house sparrow, *Passer domesticus*, better known to Americans as the English sparrow, came to the United States for the first time in 1850. Eight pairs were deliberately imported from England by a group of eminent Brooklyn gentlemen, who apparently acted from a mixture of motives. First and foremost, they thought the birds would help control such problem insects as span-worms and the caterpillar of the snow-white linden moth (*Eunomos subsignarius*) that was stripping trees at the time and had the unpleasant habit of dropping on to people's heads. But they also regarded sparrows as attractive, and a worthwhile addition to America's fauna. After all, every gardener and farmer had a problem with bugs, and a few more birds – especially jolly hardworking little insectivores like these – ought to be welcome.

The first eight pairs didn't survive, but two years later a second, larger, contingent was released in Greenwood Cemetery and 'did well and multiplied,' according to one of the importers. Supplemented by more shipments from Europe, within ten years English sparrows were chirping in half a dozen eastern cities, Enthusiasm for the birds raged unchecked. Homesick recent immigrants from the old countries of Europe were delighted to see them; as tales of sparrows' insect-killing abilities spread, more and more towns wanted birds of their own. New shipments arrived from Britain and Germany – the price climbed so high that it was sometimes actually cheaper to buy sparrows from Europe than from the rapidly expanding but jealously protected local supply. From Philadelphia (where at least 1,000 birds were released) to Maryland, West Virginia, Ohio, Kentucky, Illinois, even Texas, sparrows colonized the country. San Francisco in 1871, Salt Lake City in 1873 . . . there seemed to be no end to it. And soon the birds were moving out on their own, often hitching rides in train carriages across the expanses of the Great Plains.

'From this time to the present,' wrote Walter Barrows gloomily in his classic post-introduction survey *The English Sparrow in North America* (1883), 'the marvellous rapidity of the sparrow's multiplication, the surpassing swiftness of its extension, and the prodigious size of the area it has overspread are without parallel in the history of any bird'. It was by now absolutely clear, at least to Barrows and the great majority of his 3,000 plus survey respondents, that the whole enterprise had been a very bad idea indeed. The sparrows had, as predicted, consumed the linden moth caterpillars, but they then had no taste for the tussock moth caterpillars that took over the job of stripping trees; they were considerably more fond of grain than they were of insects, consuming up to eight pounds a year each; they attacked and drove out native bird species, including more efficient insect-eaters; and they bred like billy-o, infesting buildings, polluting parks with droppings, and generally acting like hoodlums. Gardeners found them nipping buds, mutilating fruit, and even pecking flower and vegetable seeds out of the ground the minute they were planted. Except in harvest time, moreover, they tended to stay clear of farms where they might do some good, settling instead in towns and suburbs.

As early as the 1870s, joy was turning to sorrow. A few warning voices had been raised, among them that of the great ornithologist Elliott Coues, but these had been ignored in the face of sentimental defences by sparrow sympathizers like Thomas Brewer, who in an 1868 *Atlantic Monthly* article heaped praise on 'these attractive little favourites of Young New York', meanwhile suggesting that Coues was a liar. But whereas Longfellow had hymned 'the wingéd wardens of your farms . . . Crushing the beetle in his coat of mail/And crying havoc on the slug and snail', a general U-turn now took place. Nothing bad enough could be said about sparrows. They were accused of a dismaying variety of crimes (including murder and, when sparks from foundries in Pottsville, Pennsylvania, set fire to their large ragged nests, arson). Walter Barrows's huge survey, conducted under the auspices of the Department of Agriculture, summarized the anti-sparrow position in staggering detail, concluding with a series of bloodthirsty recommendations for extermination (poisoning, snaring, repeal of protective laws, shooting, and egg-destruction; an Indianapolis marksman contributed a note pointing out that sparrows made excellent trap-shooting targets, and someone else recommended sparrow pot-pies).

Of course, nothing worked. In spite of large-scale killings, English sparrows remain today the commonest birds in the United States. Their numbers have fallen from the days when horse droppings on city streets provided them with a dependable diet of grain, but they still prefer town life to the vagaries of the country food supply, and are unlikely ever to abandon the North American continent to a more agreeable species. They don't do much good in gardens, and probably know they aren't wanted. But it's unlikely that anybody harbours quite the same degree of ill-will toward them as a century ago. 'I imagine no live Yankee would wish now to be without the life and animation of the house sparrow in his great cities,' wrote a bemused sparrow fan in 1877, and, Yankee or not, I can't totally disagree. At 6:30 in the morning, I'd trade my alarm-clock pheasant for a sparrow any day.

P.S. For those inclined to tinker with nature, a cautionary note: apart from the English sparrow, only one bird has ever been successfully introduced into North America – that other menace, the starling.

'American Weeds'

I REALIZED TO MY SURPRISE the other day that I have been trying (and incidentally failing) to grow an American Garden. It is no big deal – at the moment it consists only of a mountain laurel, an azalea, and three highbush blueberries. All are alive, but only barely, having been retrieved from the brink of terminal chlorosis more than once with a heavy dose of Miracid.

When I installed this collection on the edge of the larch wood a few years ago, I did so with nothing more than nostalgia in mind, and possibly the happy memory of eating blueberry slump in the New England Berkshires. That the plants (like me) were American natives passed through my mind, but it never occurred to me to make anything of it. And though I recognized that they all preferred acid soil conditions, that too seemed to be purely a matter of accident.

I now learn that what we have here is at least the nucleus of a garden type that for more than a hundred years, starting in the late eighteenth-century, played a role of some importance in British horticulture and garden design. In the beginning, the American Garden was at least partly responsible for bringing home the blossoms so high-handedly banished by the great landscaper 'Capability' Brown; in its later life it saw the vast and colourful development of rhododendron and azalea culture. By that time, of course, it was scarcely American at all, but a motley mixture of plants from all over the world unified mainly by their common hatred of chalk.

The earliest American Gardens were made to accommodate species coming in from the New World – kalmias, azaleas, rhododendrons, low ground covers like wintergreen (*Gaultheria procumbens*), cassiopes and bog rosemary (*Andromeda polifolia*). All of them seemed to like peaty, boggy, acid earth; there has been speculation that the first explorers, travelling along river valleys, naturally came upon such plants there. (As mountain laurel (*Kalmia latifolia*) is mostly found on hillsides in low mountains, I question this theory, but I haven't got a better one to offer.) Seeds and plants gathered by men like John Bartram (see pages 000), working largely along the Eastern seaboard from New England to Georgia, had been flooding into England, to be snapped up by connoisseurs. So many American plants were available by the 1760s, in fact, that Sir William Chambers could speak derisively of 'American weeds' when attacking the work of 'Capability' Brown.

It was Brown's successor Humphry Repton, however, who made a real virtue out of the 'weeds'. Repton realized that many of his clients enjoyed flowers, provided they could be brought back into the landscape scene in an interesting fashion. That the term 'American' still had overtones of the savage or wild did no harm in those days around the turn of the century when the taste for the picturesque ran strong. So where Brown had depended mainly upon sweeping – and empty – expanses of lawn studded with trees for his effects, Repton was driven to add excitement in other ways. These included separate smaller gardens that could be enjoyed independently, and many of them – as at Woburn Abbey, Bulstrode and Ashridge – were American Gardens. (At Ashridge, Repton actually proposed building fifteen different gardens, among them a winter garden and a medieval monk's garden, in addition to the American Garden.) As the fashion for and the availability of New World plants spread, other designers followed suit. The nurseryman Lewis Kennedy of Hammersmith built American Gardens at several estates in the home counties. At Fonthill Abbey, his vast and killingly expensive estate in Wiltshire, the eccentric William Beckford made what he called an American Plantation above the lake. It featured a large collection of flowering American trees and shrubs such as magnolias, robinias, liquidambars, azaleas and rhododendrons.

Though at first they were not very interesting – mostly unexciting shades of pink or mauve – rhododendrons were destined to become the stars and the nemeses of the American Garden. Peter Collinson had introduced the first American variety in 1736, the Carolina rosebay (*R. maximum*), planting it in his garden in Peckham, and more followed. Somewhere around the 1760s or 70s (reports differ) *R. ponticum* – not from America but the Black Sea coast of Turkey (probably via Portugal) – opened its gross purple blooms in England for the first time. *R. catawbiense* (actually an American ponticum) arrived in 1809, and not long after a yellow-flowered variety, *R. caucasicum* from (obviously) the Caucasus. The American Garden was becoming international, a process encouraged by the discovery that crossbreeding among rhododendron and azalea species was relatively easy, and could produce spectacular results.

In Belgium, growers crossed American azaleas (especially the pinxter flower, *R. nudiflorum*, whose pink blossoms on leafless stems in a bare early spring Appalachian wood are such a poignant sight) to create a wide variety of so-called 'Ghent' azaleas. Then, in 1820, crossbreeding of the rhododendrons proper took off in earnest with the introduction of the first in a long series of imports from East Asia, *R. arboreum* with its massive blood-red blooms. Soon plant breeders were successfully tinkering with the whole range of characteristics – size and form of bloom, fragrance, flowering schedule, hardiness, and above all colour. The Rhododendron Era, the era of display, was at hand.

It rather overwhelmed the more modest concept of the American Garden, even though as late as 1843 J. C. Loudon was proposing an American Garden as part of his design plan for Coleshill in Berkshire. But it has to be admitted that Loudon, for all his fame, was not an innovator. What passed for an American Garden during Victoria's reign tended to involve almost anything suited to acid soil – lilies, various conifers, heathers – no matter where it came from. Gradually the term itself fell into disuse and vanished.

Rhododendrons and azaleas, meanwhile, found their way out into extensive and often garish plantings, encouraged by the import of still more exotic varieties from the Himalayas, China, Tibet, Japan and the rugged no-man's-land of Upper Burma. An unassuming mountain laurel or bearberry, or even a perfumed sheet of trailing arbutus, was scarcely a match for a valley full of Lionel de Rothschild's brilliant Exbury azaleas, or a copse aglow with one of George Forrest's rhododendrons from Yunnan. (He single-handedly introduced more than 300 species.) You can see what I mean by visiting, for example, the long deep combe lying behind Lydney Park in Gloucestershire on a day in late May, when the hybrid rhododendrons are in all their blinding glory.

Perhaps it's misplaced patriotism, but I rather regret this development. It would be nice to bring back the American Garden, at least in a small way, and I'd do it myself if I could work out a way to acidify our good red Monmouthshire clay. For that matter, I can think of a number of plants that would fit in nicely without demanding acid. I don't insist on rhododendrons anyway, and we already have a large clump of R. *ponticum*, which came with the house.

We should note in this regard that rhododendron fanciers – at least the eighteenth-century ones – have something to answer for. That *ponticum*, so hopefully introduced 250 years ago, has now become a simple British weed. Its leathery leaves and purple blossoms are smothering hundreds of acres of irreplaceable heather moorland from Surrey to Snowdonia. You can hardly kill it; most animals refuse to eat it (reportedly, only llamas are willing). The National Trust has gone so far as to institute a *ponticum*-destruction program. My *ponticum* hasn't smothered anything yet, but I'm keeping an eye on it.

Big Trees

IT SOUNDED LIKE A WONDERFUL STORY when I first ran across it, and I was even more charmed by the title of the book – which I eventually tracked down – that was given as its source: *A Snuff-box Full of Trees*, by one W. D. Ellwanger.

It seems that until the 1850s, no nurseryman or tree fancier had ever tried raising a giant California sequoia (*Sequoiadendron giganteum*). The trees, in fact, were barely known. The more accessible coast redwoods (*Sequoia sempervirens*) had been reported a hundred years before, and described officially in 1795; the great Scottish plant-collector David Douglas, exploring the coast near San Francisco in 1831, spoke of them as giving the mountains 'a peculiar, I was almost going to say awful, appearance'. By the mid-1840s coast redwoods had been introduced into Britain (by way, strangely enough, of a Russian botanist in St Petersburg). But until the Gold Rush disturbed the quiet of the California mountains, their giant relatives remained in stately obscurity in remote mountain groves.

The coast redwoods might take the record for height (the tallest breach 350 feet) but the Big Trees are without doubt bigger, startlingly so. Considered the most massive all living forms, they may survive for as much as 4,000 years and in that time develop enormous bulk. The largest of all, the General Sherman Tree in Sequoia National Park, is 272 feet tall with a trunk diameter of 36 1/2 feet above wider buttress roots. The trees' native range is a narrow strip running about 200 miles along the western slope of the Sierras, at altitudes of between three and eight thousand feet.

A meat hunter named A. T. Dowd, working on contract for the Union Water Company, gets prime credit for discovering the Big Trees. Supposedly in pursuit of a bear, he wandered into the Calaveras Grove on the Stanislaus River about 150 miles east of San Francisco. His description of trunks thirty feet through was at first not widely believed, but word gradually spread through botanical circles. The trees were unquestionably the grandest growing things anyone had ever seen.

As Ellwanger tells the story, one day in 1854 an unsuccessful Fortyniner named G. D. Woodruff was reclining gloomily in a grove of giant redwoods when he realized that squirrels overhead were dismantling cones and sprinkling him with seeds. Thinking fast, he gathered enough seeds to fill a snuff-box and dispatched it – by Pony Express, naturally – to Ellwanger and Barry's Mount Hope Nurseries in Rochester, New York.

Rochester at this time, and for some years to come, was one of the greatest centres of commercial horticulture in the United States, and Ellwanger and Barry's establishment was biggest of all. Covering upwards of 500 acres, it specialized in fruit trees, vines and bushes, shipping not only to every corner of the country but also overseas. In 1872, for example, the Japanese Government bought a huge consignment of Ellwanger and Barry plants, while according to George Ellwanger, one of the founders (and father of the author of *A Snuff-box*), 'all the original orchards in California were planted from our nurseries'. What more logical place to launch the champion big tree into the gardens of America?

The nursery paid the freight charge ($25) for Woodruff's snuff-box, and planted out the seeds under glass, at 'a nice temperature of about 50 to 60 degrees'. The result, three years later (assisted by more seeds from Woodruff when many of the original ones failed to germinate), was some 4,000 plants. Ellwanger and Barry proudly advertised for sale, at one to two dollars depending on size, infant versions of 'one of the most majestic trees in the world'.

Unfortunately, the American market for majestic trees turned out to be dismally slow. Nobody seemed interested in growing Big Trees from California. Perhaps potential customers were discouraged by the fact that achieving full growth could take a thousand years or more, or it may be simply that the publicity was ineffective (the snuff-box story might have helped). In any case, Ellwanger and Barry had to look elsewhere for buyers. They found them in abundance in Britain, where something like a craze had developed for conifers in general, and for

Big Trees in particular.

Beginning in the late eighteenth century, a number of rich English land-owners had established pineta in which to grow the unfamiliar species arriving from America, Asia and Europe. Douglas's sensational discoveries, from the sugar pine (*Pinus lambertiana*) to the Douglas fir (*Pseudotsuga menziesii*) and the Monterey pine (*Pinus radiata*), encouraged the development; professional collectors shipped home quantities of seed to flourishing nurserymen; botanical magazines kept enthusiasm for the new trees at a high pitch. Interest in conifers was at a peak in Britain in when word of the giant sequoias filtered back from California.

The professionals moved into action fast. A year before Woodruff filled his snuff-box, an English plant-hunter named William Lobb, who had been collecting in California since 1849, sent specimens and seeds from the Calaveras Grove back to his employer, the Veitch nurseries in Exeter. Veitch passed on samples to botanist John Lindley, who, editorializing in *Gardeners Chronicle*, almost exploded with delight. 'What a tree is this! – of what portentous aspect and almost fabulous antiquity! . . . We have obtained the plant . . . it is a prodigious acquisition. But what is its name to be? Let it then henceforth bear the name of *Wellingtonia gigantea*. Emperors and princes have their plants, and we must not forget to place in the highest rank among them our own great warrior.'

Lindley's reference, of course, was to the Duke of Wellington, victor of Waterloo and much else, who had died in 1852. Queen Victoria promptly seconded the name. It was a shrewd and welcome move, so much so that in this heyday of imperial enthusiasm every gentleman, whether or not he possessed a pinetum, suddenly wanted a grove or avenue of *Wellingtonia*. Veitch sold hundreds at two guineas apiece (£110 today) with a discount for twelve or more, meanwhile admitting in his catalogue that although the tree was 'gigantic, ponderous, and imposing . . . it cannot be called beautiful'. Other dealers desperately sought stock wherever they could. It was here that Ellwanger and Barry came in. They had plenty, and quickly set about shipping off more than 2,000 otherwise unsellable potted Big Trees to a nurseryman in Liverpool.

The name *Wellingtonia* was not greeted eagerly everywhere. The

French, for obvious reasons, regarded it with horror; besides, a French botanist had decided that the Big Tree was, like the coast redwood, a sequoia, and preferred that name*. Back home, the American choice was *Washingtonia*, which quite apart from chauvinism had a certain logic to it in that Washington had at least liked trees, and Wellington didn't. Nor was that the end of the confusion: when first discovered, redwoods had been thought a species of *Taxodium*, so that name cropped up from time to time too. Argument over the *Wellingtonia/Washingtonia/Sequoia* went on and on until, in 1938, a taxonomist named J. T. Buchholtz finally determined that the tree had a different chromosome count from the coast redwood and thus belonged to a different genus. Its new name, suitably oversized and still unloved (W. J. Bean, in a new edition of his classic *Trees and Shrubs Hardy in the British Isles*, called it 'horrible') became *Sequoiadendron giganteum*.

In England, where the old name sticks, the *Wellingtonia* are gradually disappearing. In this climate, they do not grow to much more than a hundred feet, and tend to get struck by lightning. As Miles Hadfield notes in *Landscape with Trees*, they have 'no value as timber, and no one now plants them. Like the mansions whose presence in the distant landscape is marked by these towering, yet discreet exclamation marks, the *Wellingtonia* will fade away.' Westonbirt Arboretum in Gloucestershire still has a handsome grove, youthful at 140 years and 130 feet. A few famous avenues survive, including one planted after his death at Wellington's own estate of Stratford Saye in Hampshire.

In America, no Big Trees have ever rivalled the original ones, or are likely to. Of those that travelled east in the snuff-box, a fine grove of seven reportedly survived in Rochester at the Mount Hope Nurseries until the cold winters of 1918 and 1921, along with a few others in Boston. They are now easy to buy from specialist nurseries, but have never thrived in the eastern states. Thanks to the *Wellingtonia* fad in Britain, however, Woodruff did pretty well out of his encounter with the squirrels in the grove of big trees. In 1865, Ellwanger and Barry sent him a check for $1,030.60 as his share of the profits, which was probably a good bit more than he ever got panning gravel or chasing bears in the Gold Rush.

* After Sequoyah (1770–1843), the half-Cherokee scholar and educator who invented a written language for his people.

The Vegetable Patch

IT HAS BEEN A LONG TIME since I saw one of those one-wheel plough/cultivators, the sort of thing you could push through your vegetable garden to loosen the ground between the rows, or use to dig furrows. I think I remember finding one in the back of the barn when we bought a house in the Berkshires thirty years ago, but I don't recall ever having tried it out. It is probably now peacefully rusting away in whatever Valhalla ancient garden tools go to, provided they aren't captured *en route* by an antique dealer with an oil can and plenty of steel wool.

I suppose you can still buy a one-wheel cultivator. In fact I saw one for sale in a catalogue six or eight years ago, looking – as it crouched there among the plastic wheelbarrows and 'powered lawn-vac systems' – rather like a refugee from a time warp. For all I know they still stock them, though the competition from those handy little petrol-powered tillers must be severe. In my case, I did all the vegetable digging I wanted to with a big, efficient rotovator, which charged down the rows with such enthusiasm that more than once it went right on through the fence.

Significantly, however, my Berkshires vegetable garden, like the one I have now in Wales, would have suited a one-wheel cultivator. It was laid out in the standard American style, with beans, lettuces, tomatoes and whatnot arranged in rows that stretched from one end of the patch to the other. You could walk down between the odd rows, hoeing and raking, no problem. The layout was so obvious, in fact, that it never occurred to me to attempt any other. Every vegetable garden I had even seen looked just like that.

Yet according to an interesting little book called *Kitchen Gardening in America* by David M. Tucker (Iowa State University Press, 1993), planting in rows this way is not, historically speaking, standard at all.

The European style, especially in England and France, called for small solid beds, often raised, divided by paths running diagonally or at right angles. Some planting plans for vegetables in old garden books resemble geometric puzzles; even the simplest would never have admitted a rotovator. Or a horse and plough, or even a one-wheel cultivator, for that matter. On the other hand, they could be dug readily by a man with a spade, and cultivated by hand with ease. They also allowed growing flowers and herbs, even perennial varieties that disliked being disturbed.

Tucker points out that small European beds were common in the United States until well after the Civil War, in spite of the fact that American garden writers had been recommending their abolition for years. Henry Ward Beecher, writing in 1859, came out strongly for this 'better plan', while making plain that it was a radically new idea that someone had mentioned, he couldn't recall who. 'Let the garden be an oblong, say three times as long as it is broad – and cultivate it with the *plough*. Instead of having beds, let all seeds be planted in rows running the whole length of the garden. . . . A single-horse plough will dress between the rows of the whole garden in very little time. . . . The hand-weeding in the row may be performed by women or children.' In other words, while it didn't give Mom and the kids much to look forward to, the new scheme promised to do away with a lot of heavy spade work and hoeing for Dad.

The problem, of course, was the fence. Most rural vegetable patches still needed fencing against roaming livestock – foraging pigs, grazing cows, goats and sheep. As early as 1639 the Virginia Company had been issuing stern orders to settlers to 'apply themselves to the Impaling of Orchards and Gardens'; animals, so to speak, ruled the roost, and the situation hadn't improved in 200 years. The picket fence around the property remained *de rigueur*. At the same time, however, a horse-drawn plough or cultivator needed ten to twelve feet of turning room at the end of a row, an impractical amount of waste space in a closely fenced or walled garden.

Then in the 1880s barbed wire appeared. Suddenly it was possible to fence animals *in*, instead of *out*, and remove the fence from around the garden. All at once, nearly everybody with enough land switched over to the more efficient straight-row plan. Tucker quotes a writer in the magazine *American Garden*: 'We have tried the English garden long enough; let us have an American garden for American farmers.' By the time Liberty Hyde Bailey published his little guidebook *Garden-Making* in 1898, 'the old-time garden bed' warranted nothing but disdain. It 'consumes time and labour, wastes moisture, and is more trouble and expense than it is worth'. Bailey then drove home his point with a picture of a man on his knees weeding a bed. The caption: 'Cultivating a back-ache.'

It was at this point that the one-wheel cultivator/plough/hoe came into its own. Though it had been invented in the 1840s, it took the straight row to make it popular. Besides, plenty of gardeners, especially in towns, didn't have a horse, and their gardens were too small anyway. But with a contraption you push down the row, tilling was – at least arguably – easier. Mass-produced and widely publicized, the machines became highly popular. 'Every person having a garden should own one of these ploughs,' puffed the *Arkansas Gazette*. 'A boy of ten can keep the garden in perfect order.' You could buy one for two dollars, though ten dollars would get you a model equipped with a cultivator, rake, plough and seed drill. Some commentators even regarded it as an improvement on the horse-drawn equipage, although conservatives argued that nothing was better than a hoe. On the negative side, Bailey reports one gardener's opinion that 'the wheel-hoe is much too clumsy to allow the pursuit of an individual weed. While the operator is busy adjusting his machine . . . the quack-grass has escaped over the fence or has gone to seed.' A hoe could go straight to the heart of the matter.

No matter how it was cultivated, however, by hand, horse or one-wheeler, the typical American vegetable patch had been changed for good. David Tucker notes that among certain immigrant groups, notably the Italians who settled in cities, the old-fashioned beds survived. But elsewhere in the country the pattern of straight, open-ended rows prevailed. With the livestock now safely pastured where they couldn't do any damage, the best garden appeared to be the one most conveniently worked.

In the century since the conversion took place, several ironies have attended it. They suggest that the American vegetable garden has not yet found its final shape. The first irony involves the familiar issue of fences and animals – not cows and pigs this time, but woodchucks, rabbits, deer and other wild marauders. In New England, for example, what was open farmland in the nineteenth century is now more likely to be second-growth wilderness, crawling with destructive creatures that have to be barred from the beans and lettuces. (Can it be true, as I read somewhere, that Connecticut now has more trees than any other state? It certainly isn't short of woodchucks.) So back comes the fence, once so gladly dismantled, and with it the old problem of turning around at the end of a row. A big rotovator doesn't need the ten or twelve feet a horse and plough does, but anything less than three feet puts the fence (or your feet) in mortal peril.

A second irony lies in the fact that in recent years some of our more profound vegetable thinkers have argued (convincingly, I have to say) that closely-planted solid raised beds are not only more productive but more efficient and easier to work than rows. Such beds take a bit of building, but once you've got them organized you are less at the mercy of drought and your plants are happier. The growing soil, because it is concentrated, can be improved more thoroughly and with a smaller drain on your compost pile. Of course even a hoe, much less a one-wheel cultivator, is not much use here once planting has taken place.

But the biggest threat to the all-American straight-row vegetable patch may be aesthetic. There is nothing beautiful about it, and we are living in a time when cabbages seem to be valued less for coleslaw than for structural effect. Judging from such trend-setting recent publications as Joy Larkcom's *Creative Vegetable Gardening* and articles in our flossier gardening magazines, the fashion these days is for the classic *potager* – vegetables planted in carefully organized beds with flowers, and harvested only when the gardener or his family has reached the point of starvation. Personally, I have little sympathy with this movement, because I like to eat. I think I'll have another look for a one-wheel cultivator, and in the meantime hoe my own row as best I can.

Doctor Ward's Boxes

From my own knowledge and observation . . . I am of the opinion that one thousand plants have been lost, for one which survived the voyage to England. Plants purchased at Canton, including their chests and other necessary charges, cost six shillings and eightpence sterling each, on a fair average; consequently every plant now in England must have been introduced at the enormous expense upwards of £300.

WRITING FROM MACAO in the year 1819, at a time when £300 was indeed an 'enormous expense' (equivalent, in fact, to about £12,000 today), the plant enthusiast John Livingston had reason to be discouraged. China, he knew, was rich in wonderful plants, many of which would undoubtedly thrive in the West, but the chances of getting them there alive was sadly slim. The same was true of plants being found in a dozen other botanically fascinating parts of the world, from Australia to the Amazon.

In his history of the Royal Botanic Gardens at Kew, for which a number of plant-hunters worked, Ray Desmond makes plain the depressing facts about how difficult it was to send living specimens. Voyages from Canton on an East Indiaman could easily take six months, and longer if the ships had to move in convoy because of wartime threats. Sailors – and often sea captains too – normally resented giving up deck space to cargoes of plants, to say nothing of their reluctance to use up scarce water keeping them moist. Plants that didn't die of drought might well be killed off by the salt spray deposited on their leaves, or by exposure to wind or tropical sun. The authorities at Kew, of course, issued severe instructions but these may have not done much to cheer up the sailors. After recommending the use of poison against cockroaches and rats, for example, one order went on to declare that 'the crew must not complain if some of them who may die in the ceiling make an unpleasant smell'.

Many packing systems were tried for the purpose of shipping plants and seeds, none really successfully. Damp moss in cut-down casks, compartmented boxes and crates, closed boxes with ventilation holes, whole 'plant cabins' built into a ship. Sir Joseph Banks, the great naturalist who originated Kew's collecting program, favoured the latter, which consisted of boxes of earth in a small glasshouse on the quarterdeck. A packed plant cabin, however, could weigh as much as three tons. The first time one was employed, stuffed full of fruit trees destined for Australia in 1789, an iceberg holed the ship carrying it and the plant cabin – predictably – was the first object to be shoved overboard.

Probably the ultimate in plant cabins – and a rare example of success – was the arrangement devised for the ill-fated *HMS Bounty* under the command of Captain William Bligh to carry a cargo of breadfruit trees from Tahiti to the West Indies. The entire main saloon was converted into a sort of floating garden with a false floor into which pots could be set. A lead lining underneath caught and saved surplus water; a stove supplied heat when necessary and gratings could be opened for light. When the famous mutiny took place, the breadfruit trees – according to the hapless Bligh – were still in fine shape.

Even more ingenuity went into packing seeds. Tactics included soldering them into tins, bedding them in sand or brown sugar, coating them with wax or clay, or simply – Banks's recommendation – hanging them in muslin bags. Shipments were occasionally divided between vessels in hopes that some seeds would survive. Yet understandably, in view of the varying conditions of heat and damp aboard ship, plus the unpredictable viability of different kinds, here too failure outweighed success.

The great break came in the 1820s, though it was some years before the discovery was publicized and came into general use. A Scottish botanist named Maconochie was apparently the first to think of it in 1825, but since he didn't tell anybody, the fame (and the name) of the invention went instead to Dr Nathaniel Ward, whose first experiments with the so-called Wardian Case began around 1828. In a letter to the editor of the *Botanical Magazine* in 1836, Ward explained how he had buried the cocoon of a moth he was trying to hatch in some damp earth at the bottom of a bottle with a lid on it. Watching the bottle from day to day, he noticed how the moisture from the earth would rise and condense on the glass in the heat of the sun, only to return at night, keeping the soil from drying out in spite of no new water being added. To his surprise, shortly before the moth hatched a few spears of green appeared on the surface of the soil. They later turned out to be bits of grass and a fern, and once he had secured his moth, he let the plants grow on in the closed bottle. They thrived. In fact, they went on happily for *four years*, expiring only 'in consequence of the rusting of the tin lid covering the bottle'.

To begin with, Ward was delighted to find that he could now grow a wide variety of plants, even difficult ferns, in spite of the dismally polluted air in London's East End where he lived and practised medicine. But it was not long before he recognized that there was a further and 'most important' application for his invention: 'the conveyance of plants upon long voyages'. In cooperation with Loddiges Nursery in Hackney, a company already famous for having introduced dozens of new species from abroad, and eager for more, he developed the portable box that would become known as a Wardian Case. It was tightly glazed, with handles to carry it by and a wooden or metal base deep enough to accommodate soil or compost.

In 1833 Ward ran a serious test. At the beginning of June, he packed two of his cases full of ferns, sealed them, and sent them off to Sydney in the care of a 'zealous friend,' a sea-captain. They arrived in good order in spite of their six months at sea. For the return journey, the cases were filled with delicate Australian species, including at least one scrambling fern – *Gleichenia microphylla* – that had never survived the trip before. During the long return voyage – it took all of eight months – temperatures aboard ranged from 20° to 120°F. Yet when the cases were opened at Loddiges the ferns were found to be 'in a very healthy state'. There were even a couple of new seedlings.

To say that Dr Ward's cases revolutionized plant transport would be putting it mildly. Now it was possible not only to ship healthy plants, but also to start fresh seeds or cuttings and bring them into growth before packing. There were of course still disasters – leaky or smashed cases, overwatering before sealing, too much or not enough light, the wrong soil. Overlarge cases continued to annoy sailors required to manhandle them, with the usual results. But successes were notable, especially those of the great Oriental plant-hunter Robert Fortune. With the help of Wardian cases he not only introduced to Western gardeners such classic favorites as *Dicentra spectabilis*, Japanese anemones, *Weigela florida*, winter jasmine and dozens of others, but virtually created the Indian tea industry from scratch by collecting thousands of plants in China (sometimes surreptitiously, disguised as a Chinese) and shipping them to Calcutta. (An attempt to do the same for America failed. He shipped tea plants to Washington in Wardian cases in 1859. The plants survived, but what with the advent of the Civil War the enterprise didn't.)

Plant-hunters were not, as it turned out, the only ones pleased by Ward's discovery that plants could be sealed up under glass and continue to grow. It was also a boon to Victorian interior decorators, touching off the first – and probably most spectacular – terrarium fad. All manner of tabletop gardens began appearing in England and America, encouraged by the publication of Ward's illustrated pamphlet *On the Imitations of the Natural Conditions of Plants in Closely Glazed Cases* (1842) and the whimsy of inventive cabinetmakers. Domes, ornate gabled constructions, huge indoor conservatories, even glass replicas of famous monuments (the 'Tintern Abbey' model featured a gothic window at one end) adorned the finest parlours of London and New York and just about everywhere else. The plants of choice were invariably ferns.

I will not venture to say whether terrariums have had their day, although except for the ones in fourth-grade science classes they have always struck me as a bit creepy. No doubt aficionados still exist. But the Wardian Case seems to be a museum piece. According to Desmond, the last shipment of plants (from Fiji) in a Wardian Case took place in 1962. These days plant-hunters use polythene bags.

Sex and the Single Strawberry

L ET ME START WITH A SURPRISING fact: 140 years ago, the greatest wine-producing location in the United States was – Cincinnati, Ohio.

By the middle of the nineteenth century Cincinnati was turning out twice as much wine as California, and about a third of all the wine produced in the entire United States. Devoted mostly to the Catawba grape, a native American variety, the Cincinnati vineyards covered upwards of a thousand acres and yielded some 130,000 to 150,000 gallons a year. Much of it was sold as sparkling wine, probably a good dodge, since compared to wine made from European *Vitis vinifera* grapes, plain Catawba has never been much loved by connoisseurs. On the other hand, Catawba grapes would grow in Ohio, and *Vitis vinifera* wouldn't.

Remarkable as Cincinnati's standing as America's own little Burgundy may have been in the mid-nineteenth century, however, it didn't just happen. Along with several other horticultural achievements, any one of which would have satisfied a normal person's yearning for fame, it was largely the doing of a single extraordinary man. Nicholas Longworth, moreover, was neither a farmer or a scientist, but a lawyer, land speculator, millionaire, and authentic eccentric, who just happened to be fascinated by growing things from grapes to strawberries.

Born in New Jersey in 1782, to a Loyalist family whose property had been confiscated during the Revolution, Longworth studied law and headed west in 1804 to make a fortune for himself in Cincinnati. When he got there, the town contained only about 800 residents, but it was on the brink of a boom. Land, he could see, was the way to get rich. When a horse-thief whose acquittal he had secured offered him two copper whiskey stills in lieu of payment, he traded them to a tavernkeeper for 33 acres of what eventually became downtown Cincinnati, worth $2 million. Soon he had given up the law and was making money hand over fist by dealing in property. He was so successful that by 1850 he was said to be paying more real estate taxes than anybody in the country except the Astors. Cincinnati had become a metropolis, so pleasant that the English traveller Harriet Martineau declared it her choice as the best city in America to live in.

Longworth had his odd ways. One biographer called him 'a problem and a riddle', with 'a marked peculiarity and tenacity to his own opinions'. He purposely dressed in old and dirty clothes, pinning a row of slips on his sleeve to indicate business to be transacted that day; as each job was done, he ripped off a slip. One possibly apocryphal story had Abraham Lincoln, in Cincinnati on legal business, going to visit Longworth's garden and mistaking the owner for a workman. Longworth pocketed the dime Lincoln gave him, remarking that such tips were the only really honest money he ever made, 'being, by profession, a lawyer'.

Longworth was at least as much a horticulturist as a lawyer. From his earliest days in Ohio he had maintained an extensive garden – it eventually covered 20 acres and occupied four full-time gardeners – where he also grew fruit trees and vines for sale. A catalogue issued in 1825 listed hundreds of varieties of apples, pears, peaches, cherries and other fruit. Grapes for wine were a particular obsession: he imported dozens of European *vinifera* types in hopes of finding one that would grow in the climate of the Ohio Valley. (All succumbed, as elsewhere in the United States apart from the Pacific coast, to various endemic fungus diseases and insects.) The solution arrived in the form of a parcel of Catawba cuttings, a variety of wild *V. labrusca* first discovered and grown by John Adlum in Maryland. Hardy and productive, resistant (at least for a time) to black rot and mildew, it yielded what Longworth – and the American marketplace – regarded as an acceptable wine. The poet Henry Wadworth Longfellow went further. When Longworth sent him a sample of his vintage, he was moved to write a sixty-six-line ode to it ('Catawba wine/has a taste more divine/More dulcet, delicious and dreamy') as notable for its strained rhymes as for the fulsomeness of its flattery.

Longworth offered prizes for new grape varieties (Mark Twain's father sent him some, but won no prize) and improvements in growing techniques. He spent $60,000 (more than $1 million in today's money) on a winery. And he planted hundred of acres of vineyards on what has since become built-up urban land. 'So shut off and inaccessible was the place,' wrote his granddaughter, 'that our grandfather's habit was to retire there every Sunday, for seclusion. If it had been fifty miles from town, it could not have been more shut off from the bustle below.'

One should not get the impression that Longworth was simply lolling about with a glass of Catawba on those quiet Sundays. The evidence is that he was forever working on some new horticultural puzzle. In the autumn of 1832, for example, when an outbreak of cholera forced many inhabitants to leave town in hopes of avoiding infection, Longworth found himself deep in the woods of northern Ohio near Lake Erie. Not one to waste his time, he was poking around among some brambles when he came upon what he later called, in a letter to *The Gardener's Magazine* in London, 'the only everbearing raspberry I have ever met with'. It was the black raspberry or blackcap, a fine fruit, and one which Longworth subsequently introduced under the name Ohio Everbearing.

The major campaign of his later years, however, concerned the strawberry.

Strawberries had never been a particularly easy fruit to grow. For centuries in Europe they were simply collected in the wild, a laborious process – you had to be either very poverty-stricken or very fond of strawberries to amass more than a cup or two on a regular basis. But once cultivation and breeding began – in America, this generally involved the wild American strawberry, *Fragaria virginiana* – another problem showed itself. Particularly in the Midwest, the plants would simply not bear dependably. The climate wasn't to blame; the plants grew with admirable vigour; yet even imported European varieties like the hautbois (*F. eliator*) refused to produce fruit as they had at home. 'Many people grew strawberry plants in their gardens,' one early Illinois strawberry farmer recalled, 'but an inscrutable providence withheld the fruit.'

It was a situation tailor-made for an inquiring mind like

Longworth's. A certain farmer in the Cincinnati area, a German named Abergust, always had a splendid crop. Like many others, Abergust grew the variety called Early Hudson, but unlike the others, he had plants that weren't barren. Rival growers went so far as to salvage the thinned plants Mrs Abergust tossed out in the spring, but they were hopeless too. One day, however, one of the Abergust boys, strolling through Longworth's strawberry patch, let drop a remark: 'Mr Longworth, I reckon you won't have many berries; nearly all of your plants are males.' The boy conceded that Longworth would have a few, and pointed to the places likely to bear. Longworth marked the spots with stakes, and the boy proved to be right. Where he said berries would appear, berries did.

The answer, put most simply, was pollination. A 'perfect' or 'hermaphrodite' flower blossom has both stamens (producing pollen) and pistils (to receive it), and is thus self-fertile. The Early Hudson (and several other varieties commonly grown at the time) were pistillate – that is, unequipped with functioning (or adequately functioning) stamens. Unless you deliberately scattered suitable staminate plants among your pistillate plants, there was little chance of adequate pollination – or nice red strawberries. On the other hand, if your variety was predominantly staminate – male – as Longworth's apparently were, success is even more unlikely. Abergust's secret had been to plant a calculated number of male (staminate) plants of other varieties among his mainly female (pistillate) Early Hudsons.

The discovery was not a radically new one; a brilliant young French botanist named Antoine Duchesne had described the sexual variation of cultivated strawberries nearly a hundred years before. But the news had scarcely gone beyond France. Longworth's epiphany occurred in 1834. Within ten years Cincinnati was producing more strawberries than anywhere else in the world. The price dropped from 37 cents a quart to five or six cents. Poor Abergust, furious (Longworth reported that he was 'abusing his son and heaping "donner and blitzen" on my head'), gave up on strawberries and raised vegetables instead.

In spite of the theory's evident success, bitter arguments over the true nature of strawberry sex continued for years. Many horticulturists maintained (as had Linnaeus) that all strawberries were perfect.

Sterility was purely a matter of poor cultivation, or of climate. C. H. Hovey, breeder of the first important American variety, claimed that his own Hovey's Seedling had been perfect at first, but degenerated into a pistillate form over generations. Longworth, writing letters and articles, organizing committees and issuing reports, was in the thick of the battle, which came to be known as 'The Strawberry War'. His position, stated with finality in a document published by the Cincinnati Horticultural Society in 1854, was that plants were either pistillate or staminate or perfect, and stayed that way no matter what. Moreover, the only way to get a good strawberry was to plant male and female together. There was no point in trying to develop a perfect or hermaphrodite self-fertile variety.

If only because strawberry production suddenly boomed unstoppably in America, Longworth won his war. Later research revealed new complexities – strawberry gender was far more variable than recognized, with a whole sexual spectrum (sometimes hard to distinguish) ranging from male to female, and could in fact be influenced by climate. The development of hermaphrodite plants was hardly a waste of time – when he was nearly 70 Longworth himself hybridized a fine perfect variety called Longworth's Prolific that was still being grown half a century later. Virtually all modern strawberries are hermaphrodite, so there's no need to hunt for stamens and pistils.

And Longworth's prized Catawba? In the 1850s black rot and mildew devastated his vineyards and reduced Cincinnati to a very minor player in the wine world. Some forty wineries still survive in Ohio, mostly along the shores of Lake Erie.

The Mulberry Bubble

T HE FIRST, AND JUST ABOUT the only, mulberry tree I've ever been closely acquainted with stood on a low hillside in the waste land behind Roosevelt School in Ypsilanti, Michigan about sixty years ago. My very closest acquaintance with this particular tree occurred when I ran into it on a toboggan, but I also seem to recall eating excessively seed-filled berries from it in the summertime. The berries were an unappetizing white, reminiscent of maggots and tasting of nothing in particular. Compared to the self-sown apple trees on the other side of the hill, the mulberry had little to recommend it.

I now realize that I was approaching that tree in the wrong spirit altogether. Instead of clambering all over it (its branches were low) and fussing about the fact that it obstructed an otherwise excellent toboggan run, I might better have recognized it as an honourable reminder of the time when a near relative was probably the most expensive tree in the world. The most expensive mulberry, anyway.

It all had to do with producing silk. From the very beginning, European settlers in America dreamed of the riches to be made from this rare and delicate fabric. All you needed were silkworms (actually cocoon-spinning moths, primarily *Bombyx mori*) and mulberry leaves to feed them. Within a decade of the Conquest Cortés had planted mulberry trees in Mexico and imported silkworm eggs; a principal attraction of Virginia at the start of the seventeenth century, taking unfortunate precedence over the need for the colonists to figure out how to feed themselves, was the reported abundance of mulberry trees. That these turned out to be the wrong kind – the native American *Morus rubra* instead of the choice *Morus alba*, which the silkworms preferred – was all too typical of the way the silken dream kept receding.

But attempts continued, over and over again. Landing his first boatload of settlers in Georgia in 1733, General Oglethorpe promptly laid out a ten-acre garden of *Morus alba*, which just as promptly failed; John Wesley, visiting in 1737, observed that 'half the trees are dead'. In South Carolina, Eliza Pinckney, who had a famous garden with mulberry trees, actually succeeded in producing enough silk to make three dresses; meanwhile small farmers elsewhere in the South began exporting modest amounts of raw silk to England. Government encouragement in the form of bounties, some illogically high, kept the industry alive. The Revolution, however, put an end all such efforts, including, among other projects, a filature (reeling factory) that Benjamin Franklin was at the time promoting in Philadelphia.

With the return of peace, bread was needed more than silk, wheat more than mulberry trees. But by the 1820s and early 1830s, undeterred by earlier failures, enthusiasm for silk culture took off in earnest. In 1828, at the request of Congress, the Secretary of the Treasury issued a detailed 220-page manual on raising silkworms and producing silk thread; 6,000 copies sold almost overnight. Other books on the subject poured off the presses – at least eighteen between 1818 and 1844. As for magazines, the ambitious sericulturist could choose between *The Silkworm* (published in Albany every month), *The Albany Cultivator* (also Albany), *The Silk Manual and Farmer* (Boston), or *Silk Culturist* (New York). And if he wanted something a little more specialized, there were translations from distinguished foreign authorities, such as *Hints on the Cultivation of the Mulberry* by Signor Tenelli, billed as Doctor of Civil Law in the University of Pavia. Significantly, nursery catalogues contained more about mulberries than about any other fruit.

Like the 1920s, the 1830s in the United States were boom years. There was a general sense of financial excitement in the air, fuelled by soaring land prices as the government unloaded western lands, often on credit terms. Everybody seemed to be winning. Like the 1920s, too, the 1830s were heading for a fall, but at the start this did not seem obvious. Nor did it seem likely that for a fair number of people, farmers and others, a tree would be the precipitating factor.

One Gideon B. Smith of Baltimore claimed to have been the first person in the United States to raise *Morus multicaulis* (now *Morus alba* var. *multicaulis*), a shrub-like variety of mulberry that apparently originated in southern China and reached Maryland in 1826 by way of the Philippines and France. According to dazzled reports, *multicaulis* (meaning 'many-stemmed') was the magic ingredient the silk industry had been waiting for. It was said to grow with amazing speed, producing large, thin, tender and succulent leaves, perfect silkworm food. It could be cultivated conveniently as a bush.

Soon the literature was awash with stories praising *multicaulis* and advising farmers to plant it. A manual published by the Massachusetts legislature went through four editions and spread the fame of the mulberry throughout New England and beyond. State bounties offered further encouragement to establish plantations of it, not that encouragement was needed; in one remarkable case a New York businessman was given 252 acres of federal land free on the condition that he would plant 100,000 mulberry trees and provide enough silkworms to eat the leaves.

In 1837 panic struck. Banks collapsed all over the country, crippling the American economy. But the disaster seems to have done nothing to cool the excitement over mulberries. On the contrary. To those caught up in the turmoil, sericulture apparently looked like a safer investment than a quarter-section of Kansas.

In 1832, an entrepreneur named Samuel Whitmarsh had set up a silk reeling operation in Massachusetts and planted a number of acres of *multicaulis* to supply leaves. Things didn't work out for Whitmarsh; in 1838, after producing no more than a couple of black silk waistcoats and some watch ribbons, his business collapsed, leaving him with a lot of spare mulberries. It was then that he had the wit to realize that however tough making silk might be, selling mulberry trees was easy. After all, you could (so the widely-circulated story went) get $1,000 worth of cocoons from a single acre of the right kind of trees – which Whitmarsh was in a position to supply.

Suddenly everybody wanted *multicaulis*. Mulberry orchards sprang up in every state of the Union. Whitmarsh disposed of his trees for a fancy profit, and continued dealing. In September 1838, 300,000 trees sold for up to 50 cents each ($9.50 or £6.70 today) in Burlington, New Jersey, and more would have gone had the sellers been willing to accept the price. Suppliers in France tripled the cost of cuttings to exporters. In Baltimore, over 22,000 mulberry cuttings dug on 15 acres of land worth only about ten dollars an acre were valued at $45,000 ($850,000 or £600,000 today). Desperate planters paid almost anything to get the trees they needed; lots were sold and resold, the price doubling each time. One year-old trees eventually sold for up to $5 ($95 or £67). In the rush to buy and plant mulberries, silk was almost forgotten; the real money was in speculating in trees. An eyewitness reported a conversation between Whitmarsh and a doctor friend in Northampton in 1839 as they 'rejoiced over the purchase of a dozen *multicaulis* cuttings, not more than two feet long, and of the thickness of a pipe-stem, for $25. "They are worth $60," exclaimed the doctor, in his enthusiasm.' Enthusiasm indeed – today, that $60 would be equivalent to almost $1200 or £850!

It couldn't last, and it didn't. Masked by the planting hysteria, the real problems associated with producing raw silk – hatching silkworms, tending them with great care, feeding them as often as every half hour, day and night, reeling the filament, and all the rest of it – had been overlooked or sadly played down. The promised returns never materialized. Worse, the 'golden tree' turned out to be more delicate than its boosters knew, too tender even for a warm winter on Long Island, and susceptible to a mysterious blight. Late in 1838, an over-sanguine mulberry dealer dispatched an agent to France with $80,000 and instructions to buy a million *multicaulis*; by the time he got back with his precious cargo in the spring, the bottom had dropped out of the market. Totally bankrupted, the dealer was reduced to trying (and failing) to sell the trees as pea sticks for a cent apiece.

It was the end for the United States as a primary silk producer, in spite of a scattering of later efforts by state governments (particularly California) to create an industry, and smaller booms in the planting of plain white mulberry trees, *Morus alba*. Instead, with its superior technology America became a principal manufacturer of silk textiles and other products made from imported raw silk, but the day of *Morus multicaulis* was past. Cold winters and blight in the early 1840s killed off those few remaining trees that furious and frustrated farmers hadn't already grubbed up.

I don't suppose there are many silkworms chewing any sort of mulberry leaves in Michigan these days (most likely fall webworms, if anything), though I'm sure that Washtenaw County once entertained the same foolish hopes for *multicaulis* as the rest of the country. Whatever *Morus* are still around have to make their own excuse for existence. I can't help thinking, though, that my mulberry (if it survives, which I doubt) deserves just a little more respect than I ever gave it – if only for the sake of the bubble that burst.

Index

Index